Planet Earth

FOREST

Other Publications:

THE CIVIL WAR
COLLECTOR'S LIBRARY OF THE CIVIL WAR
LIBRARY OF HEALTH
CLASSICS OF THE OLD WEST
THE EPIC OF FLIGHT
THE GOOD COOK
THE SEAFARERS
WORLD WAR II
HOME REPAIR AND IMPROVEMENT
THE OLD WEST
LIFE LIBRARY OF PHOTOGRAPHY (revised)
LIFE SCIENCE LIBRARY (revised)

For information on and a full description of any of
the Time-Life Books series listed above, please write:
   Reader Information
   Time-Life Books
   541 North Fairbanks Court
   Chicago, Illinois 60611

This volume is one of a series that examines the
workings of the planet earth, from the geological
wonders of its continents to the marvels of its
atmosphere and its ocean depths.

Cover
Moss-covered tree trunks and lush growth
attest to the abundant rainfall and mild climate
of Washington State's Olympic National
Park, site of the only true rain forest in the
North American Temperate Zone.

Planet Earth

FOREST

By Jake Page
and The Editors of Time-Life Books

Time-Life Books, Alexandria, Virginia

Time-Life Books Inc.
is a wholly owned subsidiary of

TIME INCORPORATED

FOUNDER: Henry R. Luce 1898-1967

Editor-in-Chief: Henry Anatole Grunwald
President: J. Richard Munro
Chairman of the Board: Ralph P. Davidson
Executive Vice President: Clifford J. Grum
Editorial Director: Ralph Graves
Group Vice President, Books: Joan D. Manley

TIME-LIFE BOOKS INC.

EDITOR: George Constable
Executive Editor: George Daniels
Director of Design: Louis Klein
Board of Editors: Dale M. Brown, Thomas A. Lewis,
Martin Mann, Robert G. Mason, Ellen Phillips,
Gerry Schremp, Gerald Simons, Rosalind Stubenberg,
Kit van Tulleken
Director of Administration: David L. Harrison
Director of Research: Carolyn L. Sackett
Director of Photography: John Conrad Weiser

PRESIDENT: Reginald K. Brack Jr.
Assistant to the President: Juanita T. James
Executive Vice President: John Steven Maxwell
Senior Vice President: William Henry
Vice Presidents: George Artandi, Stephen L. Bair,
Peter G. Barnes, John L. Canova, Beatrice T. Dobie,
Christopher T. Linen, James L. Mercer,
Paul R. Stewart

PLANET EARTH

EDITOR: Thomas A. Lewis
Deputy Editor: Russell B. Adams Jr.
Designer: Albert Sherman
Chief Researchers: Pat S. Good, Patti H. Cass

Editorial Staff for *Forest*
Associate Editors: William C. Banks (text);
Marion F. Briggs (pictures)
Text Editors: Sarah Brash, Jan Leslie Cook
Staff Writer: Tim Appenzeller
Researchers: Susan S. Blair, Stephanie Lewis
(principals), Melva Morgan Holloman,
Gregory McGruder, Barbara Moir, Marilyn Murphy
Assistant Designer: Susan K. White
Copy Coordinators: Margery A. duMond,
Elizabeth Graham, Anthony K. Pordes
Picture Coordinator: Renée DeSandies
Editorial Assistant: Caroline A. Boubin

Editorial Operations
Design: Anne B. Landry (art coordinator);
James J. Cox (quality control)
Research: Jane Edwin (assistant director),
Louise D. Forstall
Copy Room: Diane Ullius (director),
Celia Beattie
Production: Feliciano Madrid (director),
Gordon E. Buck, Peter Inchauteguiz

Correspondents: Elisabeth Kraemer (Bonn);
Margot Hapgood, Dorothy Bacon (London);
Miriam Hsia, Lucy T. Voulgaris (New York);
Maria Vincenza Aloisi, Josephine du Brusle (Paris);
Ann Natanson (Rome). Valuable assistance was also
provided by: Janny Hovinga (Amsterdam); Gail
Cameron Westcott (Atlanta); Bob Gilmore
(Auckland); Jim Florcruz (Beijing); Lois Lorimer
(Copenhagen); Lance Keyworth (Helsinki); Bing
Wong (Hong Kong); Lesley Coleman (London);
Cheryl Crooks (Los Angeles); John Dunn
(Melbourne); David Hessekiel (Mexico City); Felix
Rosenthal (Moscow); Carolyn Chubet (New York);
Ann Wise (Rome).

Library of Congress Cataloguing in Publication Data
Page, Jake.
   Forest.
   (Planet earth)
   Bibliography: p.
   Includes index.
   1. Forest ecology. 2. Forest and forestry. 3. Trees.
I. Time-Life Books. II. Title. III. Series.
QK938.F6P25 1983   582.16'052642   83-624
ISBN 0-8094-4344-9
ISBN 0-8094-4345-7 (lib. bdg.)

THE AUTHOR

Jake Page is a contributing editor and columnist
for *Science '83*. He was formerly the editor of
Natural History magazine, has served as science
editor of *Smithsonian* magazine and was the original director of Smithsonian Books. He has writ-
ten extensively about environmental sciences and
natural history, including an exhaustive study of
one of America's most ancient Indian tribes,
Hopi, which he co-authored with his wife, photographer Susanne Page.

THE CONSULTANTS

Dr. Edward S. Ayensu is Director of the Smithsonian Institution's Office of Biological Conservation and Secretary General of the International
Union of Biological Sciences. An authority on
the conservation of renewable resources, especially in developing countries, his research inter-
ests include tropical deforestation, desertifica-
tion and fuel-wood supply, endangered species
and habitats, medicinal plants of the world, and
the utilization of science and technology for development. Dr. Ayensu is the author and editor
of many books and scientific articles, including
Jungles, The Rhythms of Life and *Endangered or
Threatened Plants of the United States.*

Dr. Theodore T. Kozlowski is Director of the
University of Wisconsin's world-renowned Bio-
tron, a controlled-environment facility for the
study of plants and animals. He is also a professor in the Department of Forestry and has done
extensive research on the effects of environmental stresses on trees. He is the author and co-
author of more than 20 books covering this field.

Francis M. Hueber is Curator of Paleobotany at
the Smithsonian Institution's National Museum
of Natural History. Although his specialty is
the fossil evidence of the evolution of early
land plants, his studies also include fossil ferns,
plants preserved in amber, and plant remains
found in excavations of the ruins of Pompeii.

CONTENTS

THE MANY FACES OF THE FOREST

The forests that cloak 30 per cent of the earth's land area are testimony to Charles Darwin's marveling declaration in 1859 that "endless forms most beautiful and most wonderful have been, and are being, evolved." Across the planet, tens of thousands of different tree species have conquered almost every kind of climate and terrain.

On a global scale, variation in the world's forests follows regular patterns. Broad belts of conifers in high latitudes give way to broad-leaved deciduous trees in temperate regions, and these woodlands in turn blend into expanses of lush rain forest in the tropics. Locally, small variations in precipitation, topography, and soil type result in forests of startlingly different aspect. A few miles north of dense stands of subarctic evergreens, a slightly harsher climate reduces the same tree species to scattered, gnarled shrubs that may live more than a century without attaining the height of a human adult.

The innumerable environments of the middle latitudes produce forest variations ranging from expanses of leatheryleaved scrub in arid country to pockets of lush rain forest where the temperate zone masquerades as the tropics. Even tropical rain forest is no uniform riot of green, but is subtly differentiated into forms that include the high-canopied lowland jungle, its floor so shady that little undergrowth takes root, and the stunted cloud forest, choked with undergrowth, of tropical mountainsides.

A few forests even lack conventional trees. In some temperate and tropical deserts, ordinarily low-growing cacti have evolved woody trunks and treelike stature, creating a sere forest where no broadleaf or conifer could survive.

For all its variety, the global tapestry of forests has one universal characteristic: Every forest dominates its landscape and shapes the existence of every plant and animal living in its shadows. The forest, in all its guises, is as much a part of the earth's geography as features of geology and terrain.

A rainbow shimmers above the widely scattered spruce trees of one of the northernmost of forests, in Denali National Monument, Alaska. Because the annual growing seasons last no more than three months, trees here are limited to heights of 10 to 15 feet.

A rain forest in the mountains of New South
Wales, Australia, injects a scene of tropical
lushness into a temperate region. An average
annual rainfall of 85 inches fosters the luxuriant
growth of a variety of ferns and mosses.

A winter finery of ice clothes the boughs of a
cypress forest fringing a lake in Illinois. These
bald cypress trees, common in the swamps
and bayous of the American South, are growing
at the northernmost extreme of their range.

A beech forest in northeast Japan spreads fragile new leaves above a snow cover that has lingered into May. All temperate broad-leaved forests shed and regrow their foliage in response to the changing seasons, and some tropical forests are also deciduous, losing their leaves during dry spells and budding with the onset of rainy weather.

The seamed trunks of tree cacti rise from stony ground on Santa Fe Island, in the Galápagos. Here and in other arid parts of South and North America, some cactus species grow to heights that exceed 60 feet.

Widely spaced live oaks dot a tawny California hillside. Like most other trees found in sparse savanna and chaparral woodland, the oaks have small, glossy leaves and thick bark that retain moisture during long dry spells.

3,000 feet high on a Mexican mountainside.
Found in cool, damp tropical highlands, cloud
forests are characterized by low-crowned trees
heavily overgrown with vegetation.

Chapter 1

THE LEGACY OF WILDFIRE

At twenty minutes before eleven o'clock on the night of August 23, 1967, a lookout scanning the forest on Idaho's Sundance Mountain spotted the first telltale glow of a fire. He was neither surprised nor alarmed; it was the height of the fire season, and a small army of well-trained and well-equipped fire fighters was poised nearby to attack the slightest flame.

The danger had been increasing steadily since May. Barely one tenth of an inch of rain had fallen on Sundance Mountain over the past two months, and all during August the fire hazard had been classified as "extreme" throughout 150,000 square miles of wilderness in Oregon, Washington, Montana and Idaho. Since the beginning of the month, a high-pressure system—a mass of clear, dry air—had been stalled over the Northwestern United States, blocking the moist Pacific Ocean air that usually brought some showers to the area at this time of year. Temperatures had been approaching 100° F. every day, the relative humidity was hovering at about 30 per cent—not much higher than the mean annual reading in California's Death Valley—and the moisture content of the trees and the organic litter on the forest floor was alarmingly depleted. According to the records kept at the Priest River Experimental Forest about 25 miles from Sundance Mountain, fallen trees lying on the ground had become as flammable as seasoned kindling.

For weeks, sharp-eyed lookouts had been scanning the forest continuously from some 200 stations towering above the rolling carpet of evergreens. Small airplanes had been droning back and forth overhead, carrying infrared scanners capable of detecting the heat of even a small campfire. Powerful bulldozers, sophisticated communications equipment and even a squadron of vintage World War II bombers loaded with fire-retardant chemicals had been deployed in the area, and a veteran company of fire-fighting paratroops, known as smokejumpers, was standing by.

There had even been occasion to practice. Thus far in August, lightning had ignited four fires on or near Sundance Mountain. One had required 37 men, including a squad of smokejumpers, to control it, but all the fires had been outrun, outflanked and outfought by the determined fire fighters. On this quiet, late-summer night, the tiny orange glow of flame near a stream called Soldier Creek seemed as likely to succumb to human intervention as the blazes that had gone before.

The fire fighters went to work confidently, but with a sense of urgency because of a different kind of threat contained in the weather report: The torpid high-pressure area was giving way to a low-pressure storm system

A column of flame consumes a stand of fir trees during a fire that burned 650 acres in Idaho. A crown fire such as this, which leaps from treetop to treetop, is the fastest-spreading and most destructive sort of forest conflagration.

now approaching the Washington coastline: Winds in northern Idaho were expected to be as high as 25 miles per hour.

Working all night and long into the next day, hosing down the flames with water pumped from tanker trucks, clearing away flammable undergrowth and hacking out firebreaks, the fire fighters limited the extent of the blaze to 35 acres. Although the fire was considered to be under control—no longer spreading—it was not yet out. The crews spent the next five days dousing burning logs and stumps with water and chemical fire retardants while bulldozers stripped all flammable material from eight-foot-wide firebreaks surrounding the charred area. By that time some 300 men were involved, and the worst injury reported so far had been a bee sting.

Then, at 10:20 p.m. on August 29, the fire flared anew. Impelled by a northeast wind and by the normal downslope flow of cooling nighttime air, the fire jumped the line and roared down the mountainside, out of control. The fire fighters, ordered to retreat, fled with their equipment as the flames leaped from the brush into the crowns of the trees, feeding voraciously on the oily needles and advancing at nearly a mile an hour.

Bulldozers tried to clear a firebreak wide enough to halt the flames, but the fire continued its implacable spread. After two days of struggle, the fire fighters asked the United States Forest Service for help. For a few hours after the reinforcements arrived on September 1, the crews seemed on the verge of getting the fire under control. But as the day progressed the wind began to rise, and the expansion of the flames accelerated. In a matter of hours, it was clear that another major run was under way. During the afternoon and early evening, the flames consumed nearly 12,000 acres of forest. A great column of smoke rose thousands of feet into the sky, a visible sign of the fire-induced convection currents that, together with the wind, lofted fire-brands—burning coals, branches, chunks of bark and pine cones—as far as 10 miles ahead of the conflagration, where the spot fires thus ignited soon combined into fierce progeny of the main fire.

Despite the rapid spread of the flames, there was no stampede of wildlife. In fact, the creatures of the forest generally escape even a major fire such as this one, and the crews noticed few if any signs of life amid the dense smoke and intense heat. Deer and other fleet-footed forest dwellers had long since fled; even the snakes had slithered to safety. Because they were determined to stand and fight, it was the fire fighters who were in the gravest danger: At about 6 p.m., two of them died beneath a bulldozer where they had huddled for shelter when overtaken by the flames and searing winds.

Late in the day, as it began to climb a ridge called the Selkirk Divide, the fire slowed its advance, but firebrands were still being cast ahead, and the flames gradually licked up the side of the divide after them. The column of smoke, now 25,000 feet high, was visible on radar screens in Missoula, Montana, nearly 200 miles away across the mountains. Fire-induced winds reached speeds of 80 miles an hour and blew down entire stands of trees.

Realizing that no amount of effort could check the blaze, the fire fighters withdrew to temporary camps while the flames ran their course. Lookouts around the perimeter of the fire maintained continuous radio contact with strategists at the United States Forest Service field headquarters in nearby Sandpoint, Idaho. By coordinating reports from the front, the headquarters staff could figure out what the fire was doing and make predictions about where it might go next. As evening fell, the fire front—now four miles

Photographed at a distance of just 200 feet, a bolt of lightning slashes into an ash tree. Although lightning injures many thousands of trees each year and touches off a significant proportion of all forest fires, this stroke left the ash undamaged—perhaps because a thin film of rain water on the tree's bark conducted the discharge to the ground.

IGNITION

AFTER 3 MINUTES

AFTER 4 MINUTES

AFTER 5½ MINUTES

AFTER 10 MINUTES

AFTER 12 MINUTES

A sequence of photographs taken during a fire in Glacier National Park, Montana, charts the rapid growth of a spot fire that was kindled by a brand lofted from the nearby main blaze. Fanned by hot, dry winds, the tiny blaze swelled into a crown fire within four minutes *(center left)*; after 12 minutes *(bottom right)*, the advancing flames had burned a half-mile stretch of forest.

20

wide—was approaching the Pack River, northeast of the divide. There, confounded by the fickle winds in the sheltered drainage area near the river, the fire front stalled temporarily.

For a while, the crews could feel no breeze at all at ground level, but they could hear the wind howling like an express train through the high branches. Soon treetops began to break off, and great whirlwinds rampaged through the area, snapping trees like toothpicks as gusts topped 95 miles per hour. Sucking monumental quantities of air into its vortex, preceded by spot fires and firebrands, propelled by the winds and the raging power of its own intense heat, the fire had become a fire storm. The moving blast furnace crossed the Pack River at about 7 p.m., igniting the beams that supported the approaches to the Pack River bridge. The bridge itself soon collapsed, and the heat was so intense that the $\frac{5}{16}$-inch-thick carbon steel plates on the bridge softened and folded over the wreckage. Later tests showed that softening this kind of steel required a temperature of 1,200° F.

The fire raced on at a rate of more than six miles per hour toward Apache Ridge to the northeast. Convection currents and radiant heat from the flames desiccated the facing slope of the ridge and heated the trees there almost to their ignition temperature. When the first sparks from the advancing fire storm touched down, the entire slope exploded into flame.

During the next three hours, the front swept over still another mountain, and spot fires broke out on a third. Then, reaching an area that had recently been harvested by a logging company, the main front ran out of fuel just as the weather began to improve; the wind decreased to about 10 miles per hour, and the relative humidity rose. Now almost 20 miles from its starting point, the front finally lost its coherence, becoming ragged and poorly defined. Fires still burning in the ravaged area were extinguished at last on the 10th of September—18 days after the lookout on Sundance Mountain had sounded the first alarm.

The Sundance fire was a giant among the many forest fires that erupted in the Northwest during the drought-plagued year of 1967, and the remarkable speed of its major run on September 1—which covered 16 miles in nine hours—remains something of a legend in the region. In all, it visited devastation on 50,000 acres, and its disastrous effects were not limited to the millions of trees destroyed outright; many others were left with wounds that provided access for the legions of insects and fungi that parasitize and eventually kill trees.

Other long-range effects were less easily discerned: Like all major forest fires, this blaze had savaged the entire forest environment, and a casualty count of the trees could only be one entry in the final damage assessment. Typically, wildfires burn with such intensity that they consume all the ground litter, exposing the soil and sharply reducing its absorbency. This leads to an immediate increase in the volume and strength of water runoff, which causes drastic land erosion. As topsoil and ash particles are washed into streams, the increased siltation diminishes water quality and harms aquatic creatures. Such damage is long lasting: Seventeen years after Oregon's great Tillamook Burn, a fire that destroyed 300,000 acres in 1933, local streams still carried as much as eight times the normal silt load.

The formidability of a fire can also be measured in terms of the human struggles against it. The Sundance fire, for example, had routed a well-organized, technologically advanced and thoroughly prepared fire-fighting

Impelled by strong updrafts of heated air, a vortex of embers twists above a forest fire in Idaho. Such fire whirls can loft firebrands 500 feet in the air and cast them into the surrounding forest to touch off new fires.

army with humiliating ease, roaring along until a fortunate combination of environmental factors gradually brought it to a stop. Its potency, in fact, immediately became part of a debate that had been going on among foresters for decades, and weighed in heavily on the side of two hotly contested notions: When conditions are right for a fire, little can be done to prevent it; and once a fire gets out of control, it will probably run its natural course regardless of human attempts to stop it.

These are sobering propositions but they are nevertheless consistent with what naturalists have long understood: All forests are highly complex ecosystems that do not take human meddling well. From the uppermost tree branches to the bedrock beneath the soil, every forest is an intricate, living mosaic that relies for its survival on subtle interdependencies born of millions of years of adaptation to environmental factors. And one of the factors that has been persistently and almost universally at play during that entire history has been wildfire. Interfering with its natural action can, it seems, be as harmful as any other kind of meddling.

Truncated and toppled trees, ghostly in the slowly clearing smoke two days after Idaho's Sundance Mountain fire, testify to the ferocity of the raging fire storm. Many of the trees were felled by winds that exceeded 95 miles an hour as superheated air rushed skyward and surrounding air swept in to replace it.

Records preserved within the trees themselves—charred wounds subsequently enfolded in new wood and preserved in the sequence of annual rings—show that fire has always been a frequent event in, for example, the pine forests of the Southeastern United States and the sequoia and ponderosa pine forests of the West. Naturally occurring fires have been less frequent, but usually far more intense, in the northern Rockies. Indeed, it is likely that with the exception of the rain forests, every square foot of the world's woodland has been burned many times. And just as they have reacted to other environmental conditions, the trees have adapted in various ways to these periodic visitations of flame.

Many trees, including pines, oaks and redwoods, have thick, insulating bark that reduces the damage done to them by fire. The deep root systems of some hickories permit rapid regeneration of a tree if a fire ravages the trunk and branches. The rapid growth of young pines lifts their foliage quickly above the reach of most low-level brush fires. Beeches, maples and basswoods have fire-resistant leaves. Sugar maples are normally highly vulnerable to fire, but because their foliage decomposes rapidly on the forest floor, little fuel accumulates there. Oaks, redwoods and chaparral recover rapidly after a fire by quickly sprouting new shoots from the charred trunks and stumps. Other trees are adapted for rapid colonization of nearby burned-over areas. Quick seed production by jack pines and lodgepole pines allows the next generation to become established immediately after a fire. The light, puffed seeds of the trembling aspen often float into a burned-out area and germinate before its competitors can take hold.

Sometimes fire helps one species of tree to dominate an entire forest. The fires that occur naturally every five to 25 years in some areas of the American West, for example, do little damage to the thick-barked, mature ponderosa pines of the region. But young ponderosas that have not yet developed thick bark cannot survive the fires and are winnowed out. If they were not, they would form dense thickets from which a fire could spread upward to the crowns and destroy the entire forest. Fires also burn off some of the ground cover, preparing a bed for seedlings. During fire-free intervals, some of the young pines have time to develop thick bark and grow to maturity, replenishing the forest gradually as the older trees die off.

In Australia, fire is in part responsible for the predominance of eucalyptus trees in the forests that fringe the coast. Thick bark not only protects the trunk tissue from ground fires but also shelters incipient buds that sprout quickly into leaf-bearing shoots. The new leaves provide food for growth, and the eucalypts flourish while other plants are still struggling to recover.

Fire can also be an agent of diversity. In the area around Sundance Mountain in Idaho, for instance, forests dominated by gigantic Douglas firs also contain a variety of other trees, albeit mostly other cone-bearing evergreens. These other trees—western larch and lodgepole pine—are less tolerant of shade than is the dominant Douglas fir, and if fires did not occur periodically, they would be crowded out of the forest when the tall firs cut off their supply of light. But as long as fires sweep through this region once every 20 years or so, the diversity of the forest is maintained.

The adaptation of some trees to frequent fire has been so thoroughgoing that they cannot reproduce without it. The cones of the lodgepole pine and the jack pine need high temperatures to melt their resin so that the seeds can escape from the cones and fall to the ground. Without fire, the seeds remain dormant for years. But the lodgepole pine is exceptionally patient; its seeds have been known to survive encased in resin for 80 years.

The consequences of a forest fire extend far beyond the trees affected. Not the least of its roles is that of aiding the decomposition of organic debris. Both in the tropics and near the Poles, the growth rate of plants seldom exceeds the rate of decay, but this is not true of the temperate latitudes. There, fire is the principal agent of decomposition. In effect, fire speeds up the process of decay by quickly releasing the nutrients stored in the leaves and twigs that accumulate on the forest floor. After one fire in a Douglas fir forest, for example, the number of plant species emerging from the ashes was twice the number observed before the fire.

In addition to enriching the soil, fires consume the litter on the forest floor, destroying the favored habitat of many tree-killing insects, and smoke from the fires discourages various kinds of fungi that parasitize trees. When large fires burn off the trees' upper foliage, more sunlight reaches the ground, encouraging the growth of plants that once languished in the sylvan gloom. In some forests, the new vegetation provides fodder for grazing animals such as deer and elk, and during the first year or so, this fodder is particularly rich in proteins, calcium and phosphates.

An important lesson about these relationships was learned in Michigan when the success of modern fire-prevention efforts almost caused the extinction of one of the rarest birds in the United States. Kirtland's warbler, a bluish gray bird with a yellow abdomen, nests only in the lower peninsula of Michigan and only in a forest dominated by jack pine, a relatively short and often bushy evergreen. The bird makes its nest in the soil near the base of the jack pine trunk, but not all trees provide bushy low branches for cover. The limbs of very young jack pines are too widely spaced to offer the

Charred by an intense wildfire, a forest of paperbark trees in Western Australia sprouts lush new foliage just a year later. Such rapid recovery is possible because the trees' thick bark protects dormant buds from flames.

necessary protection, and older trees lose the lower branches because higher ones shade them. Only jack pines from five to 18 feet tall are suitable.

The hard times for these birds began in the 1960s, when foresters intensified fire-prevention efforts in the 600-square-mile area favored by Kirtland's warblers. By publicizing good fire-prevention advice and periodically burning off the organic litter with small, controlled fires, foresters all but eliminated wildfire from the region. In 1971, bird watchers noticed a sharp decline in the Kirtland's warbler population. At that time, it was estimated that there were only about 200 males alive.

Without occasional wildfires, the jack pines had begun to grow beyond the height preferred by the warblers. Deprived of protective cover, the warblers were increasingly victimized by cowbirds, intruders that take over other birds' nests. The demise of the warbler seemed certain until ornithologists and foresters realized that the jack pine area—and the Kirtland's warbler—had evolved with fire as a constant handmaiden. Now, in tandem with efforts to get rid of cowbirds, the jack pine forests are periodically and selectively burned to make room for new trees. By early 1980, the warbler population had stabilized, but a high price was paid for this success. That spring, a fire set by foresters flared out of control, destroying 25,000 acres and 44 homes. Sifting through the remains of his house, one resident commented: "I hope that warbler enjoys his nest. My nest is burned."

Although foresters have only recently begun to fully appreciate the subtle interactions of fire and forest, there is little doubt that the aboriginal inhabitants of North America, Latin America, Africa, Eurasia and Australia all knew something of the beneficial effects of forest fires and deliberately set fire to various tracts of land. One early account suggests that small fires were sometimes started in the forest to clear away dangerous accumulations of shrubbery and flammable organic litter that might serve as kindling for a huge wildfire. Others were set to flush out game. More often, though, fire was used to prevent the forests' encroachment into open hunting grounds. In historic times—and presumably earlier—the Slave and Cree Indians of northern Alberta in Canada fired the prairies and meadows each spring to keep the forest from advancing. As a further bonus, the ash-enriched soil yielded a nutritious crop of grass and shrubs that attracted game. That some American Indians understood fire behavior well is apparent in a description recalled by an elderly Cree-Metis Indian whose tribe lived in Alberta. "See, you start a fire at the top of a meadow in the afternoon, when you feel the wind change, the way the cool air does at that time. This way the fire burns toward the low part of the meadow where all the wet grasses are. And then it just goes out. It's safe. You have to know the wind. You have to know how to use it." Not all primitive people were so methodical, however, and it is likely that many of their deliberately set fires roared out of control.

When Europeans launched their great era of exploration and colonization in the 15th Century, they used fire to clear land for farming. In 1420, Portuguese settlers burned off most of the primeval coniferous forests on the Atlantic island of Madeira, some 375 miles off the North African coast; the forests that had covered the island for thousands of years were replaced by vineyards and sugar-cane fields, and as the woodlands shrank, so did the numbers of creatures that had flourished in the forest environment. In the New World too, fire was the technique of choice for clearing farmland. But as the number of settlers increased, the practice had to be curtailed. People who had established farms and built villages did not want forest fires threatening them. And with the westward migration of European civilization came the wholesale logging of vast forested areas, to clear them for farming and to satisfy the growing demand for timber. Logging practices were brutal: Timbermen took all the trees they wanted and left great quantities of slash—treetops, branches and other waste parts—on the forest floor, ready tinder for lightning or human accident to cause a conflagration.

And conflagrations there were. In 1871, an enormous forest fire near Peshtigo, Wisconsin, claimed 1,500 lives. In 1894, more than 400 people perished in a forest fire near Hinckley, Minnesota. In 1910 a single fire razed three million acres in Idaho and Montana, destroyed several towns, and killed 85 fire fighters. Such catastrophes, and the growing awareness that the great forest resources of the nation were dwindling, pointed to an urgent need for good forest management. But there were no American forest managers at the turn of the century, and no schools of forestry.

Europeans, on the other hand, had been conscious of the need to protect forest resources ever since the great oak-hulled battleships of the 17th and 18th Centuries sallied forth in quest of empire. By the early 19th Century, centers of forestry education had been established in many European countries. But for all the valuable experiences of European forest managers, naturalists on both continents recognized that Americans would eventually have to develop programs specially tailored to the different population patterns and enormous scale of the New World's forest lands.

The name most often associated with American forestry is Gifford Pin-

Fire visits many forests almost as regularly as the seasons change. And the clearest records of its depredations are found hidden in the wood of trees that the fire scorched but did not kill, leaving scars that can be dated by correlating them with annual growth rings.

The ponderosa pine shown in cross section below endured a succession of blazes so frequent that a wound left by the first fire, in 1659, never had time to heal and acquire a new layer of bark, which might have protected the wood from subsequent fires. Instead, the damaged tissue—made even more vulnerable by the flammable pitch that oozed from the wound—was scarred again and again by recurrent fires while the rest of the trunk, protected by undamaged bark, grew apace.

Despite the damage to individual trees, forests as a whole benefit from regular wildfires. Many tree species depend on fire to germinate their seeds, to restrict competing species, to thin out stands of trees for optimum growth, and to burn off accumulations of brush and litter that might eventually fuel a catastrophic fire. Indeed, without the frequent minor blazes that scarred it, this tree and its woody chronology might long ago have been destroyed in a full-scale conflagration.

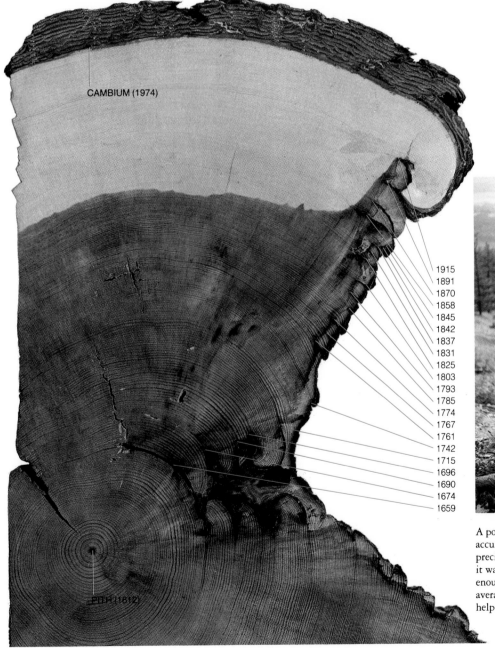

CAMBIUM (1974)

1915
1891
1870
1858
1845
1842
1837
1831
1825
1803
1793
1785
1774
1767
1761
1742
1715
1696
1690
1674
1659

PITH (1612)

A ponderosa pine hollowed by a 256-year accumulation of fire wounds (*above*) revealed a precise record of past forest fires (*left*) when it was felled and sectioned in 1974. Fires severe enough to scar the tree recurred at intervals averaging 13 years until modern fire control helped check the cycle after 1915.

chot. Raised in New York City, Pinchot was steered toward a career in forestry by his father, an ardent naturalist. After graduating from Yale in 1889, Pinchot went to Europe to pursue an education in forestry. He studied for 13 months in Germany, France and Switzerland, then returned to the United States. Refusing the offer of a job in the Department of Agriculture's small and ineffective Forestry Division, Pinchot became a forester at Biltmore, the estate of George W. Vanderbilt near Asheville, North Carolina. But eight years later, after gaining much practical experience, he accepted an offer to join the Forestry Division, this time as its chief.

Their growth made possible by fire, lodgepole pine seedlings sprout beside a fallen cone. Lodgepole cones remain closed, sometimes for as long as 25 years, until a wildfire's heat melts the resins that seal the cone scales and releases the seeds to germinate in the blackened landscape.

At that time, the division had little or no real administrative authority over the nation's vast woodlands, but the groundwork for an increased jurisdiction was laid in 1899 when Pinchot and Theodore Roosevelt, then the conservation-minded Governor of New York, became fast friends. Tall and lanky with a full and flamboyant mustache, Pinchot seemed an odd match for the burly Roosevelt, but the two men had much in common. Both came from wealthy and influential families and were outspoken conservationists, avid outdoorsmen and firm believers in healthy exercise. Pinchot recalled, "T.R. and I did a little wrestling, at which he beat me; and some boxing, during which I had the honor of knocking the future President of the United States off his very solid pins."

In 1905, with the enthusiastic backing of Roosevelt—who was by then serving his second term as President—Pinchot's organization was given full jurisdiction over all government-owned forest lands, some 86 million acres, and its name was changed to United States Forest Service. Pinchot immediately inaugurated the first large-scale attempt in North America to combine conservation practices—such as selective cutting to leave a healthy residual forest—with commercial productivity.

Pinchot was guided by a useful precedent. Some 30 years before, Yellowstone National Park had been created to preserve the nation's natural grandeur. Now, borrowing this concept, Pinchot established a number of national forests, hoping to protect the woodlands from exploitation. But conservationism was not a popular cause in the early 20th Century, and two years after Roosevelt left office in 1908, Pinchot was replaced. Neverthe-

A seedling of a wattle, a member of the acacia family, rises from the ashes of a forest fire in Australia. Acacia seeds, which are capable of lying dormant for decades, germinate only after fire splits the tough seed coats, letting moisture reach the embryonic plants.

less, he remained active in forestry all his life, and many of his precepts are still applied in national and privately owned forests throughout the world.

In Pinchot's day, one of the obvious requirements in the preservation of forest lands was the prevention of fire: "Like the question of slavery," Pinchot once noted, "the question of forest fires may be shelved for some time, at enormous cost in the end, but sooner or later it must be met." In most countries, the policy was to attack each fire with ever-increasing numbers of fire fighters until the flames were put out. The primary goal was to limit damage, and the efforts yielded substantial results. Despite the continued frequency of fires in some areas of the United States, overall fire damage has in fact been reduced since Pinchot's time. For example, tree rings in California incense cedars show fire scars approximately every eight years from the 1600s to the beginning of the 20th Century, but few since then.

Insistent public information campaigns have helped to hold down the incidence of forest fires caused by human accident. The most notable of these, launched in 1944 by the U.S. Forest Service, features Smokey the Bear, a kindly-looking brown bear decked out in a forest ranger's uniform and hat. "Only you," declares Smokey year after year, "can prevent forest fires." The message has been measurably effective; in recent years, the number of man-made forest fires on United States public lands has remained steady, despite rapid growth in the number of visitors. In West Germany, Smokey's counterpart is a caricature of a squirrel with its tail on fire. Still, fires of human origin account for thousands of wildfires every year.

The rest are started by lightning. It has been estimated that more than

Fire in the Laboratory

By kindling small fires in their laboratories, researchers in the United States and Australia are scrutinizing the chemical and physical complexities of forest fires. They are looking for ways to make wildfire easier to predict and control, and to make controlled fire a more useful tool for managing forests.

Combustion chambers packed with instruments allow scientists to analyze how the behavior of a fire changes when it is consuming various forest materials, or when it is burning in different conditions of air temperature and relative humidity. Wind tunnels and inclined test beds duplicate the effects of air movement and sloping terrain. Analysis of smoke and ash from laboratory blazes yields clues to the effects of forest fires on visibility and air quality and the role of fire in recycling nutrients in forest soils.

The U.S. Forest Service Southern Forest Fire Laboratory in Macon, Georgia, scene of the work shown here, was the first such facility in the world when it was founded in 1959. Its location was hardly coincidental; forest-fire research has long been particularly important in the American South, where controlled fire is routinely used in timber plantations and forest preserves. Applying techniques developed in the laboratory, forest managers promote healthy woodlands by deliberately burning three million acres of pine forests a year to thin undergrowth, prepare the forest floor for tree planting, reduce plant disease, and lessen the chance of later wildfires.

A bed of pine needles burns in a combustion chamber at the Southern Forest Fire Laboratory, under the electronic scrutiny of a rack of temperature sensors. Instruments in the bell-shaped hood analyze the smoke, while devices in the framework supporting the burning fuel record the weight loss due to combustion.

Flames creep down an inclined test bed in an investigation of the influence of forest fires on air quality. The slope causes the flames to lean away from the unburned pine needles, duplicating the slow spread of a prescribed fire burning against the wind.

Burning pine needles sear fronds of palmetto, a typical forest shrub in the American South, in an experiment devised to analyze smoke produced by intentional burning of undergrowth.

eight million bolts of lightning strike the earth every day. Most expend about 20 kilowatt-hours of electricity, enough to power an average American household for 24 hours, in a few millionths of a second. Not every bolt starts a fire. Sometimes it shears off a limb or splits a trunk, leaving a tree susceptible to a slow death from disease or insect infestation. One study made in the pine forests of Arkansas showed that nearly 70 per cent of all tree deaths were caused by lightning bolts that did not start fires.

But roughly one lightning bolt in 10 lasts for an extraordinarily long time—perhaps a half second. It is these superbolts, which may discharge up to 300 kilowatt-hours, that are most likely to ignite a tree. They create temperatures close to 21,000° F., far above the 752° F. temperature sufficient to kindle most wood.

A bolt searing into the soft and shaggy bark of a fir tree, for example, often tears loose burning chunks that tumble to the forest floor. After smoldering for a time amid the litter there, the glowing fragments ignite the debris. Every year, lightning starts some 50,000 forest fires worldwide, including 10,000 in the United States. If rain accompanies the lightning, many of these fires will sputter out before much damage can be done. But in hot, arid regions such as southern Australia and the American West, rain often evaporates before reaching the ground, and the so-called dry lightning that results is especially hazardous in desiccated forests.

Fires take several forms. A blaze that remains on the forest floor, burning shrubs and organic litter, is called a surface fire. Often lethal to saplings, surface fires may also kill larger, more fire-resistant trees by scorching their exposed roots. Another type of fire, the ground fire, is flameless. When peat and thick litter deposits are ignited, the fire typically burns underground, devastating tree roots and drastically altering the chemistry of the soil. Such fires are almost impossible to extinguish, even when water is plentiful. They may smolder for months, often remaining active under the snow throughout the winter. In most cases, ground fires erupt periodically into surface fires. When flames manage to climb into the tops of the the trees and ignite the foliage, the outburst is called a crown fire. Intense and highly destructive, crown fires are the fastest-moving fires of all.

Once a blaze is discovered, fire fighters can use an impressive array of techniques and technologies to put it out *(pages 36-43)*. But the expense of such efforts is staggering: By the early 1980s, the Canadian government alone was spending nearly $250 million every year to fight forest fires; in the United States, where forested areas are more populous, the expenditure was even greater, exceeding $500 million.

Faced with the ever-increasing costs of fighting fires, and recognizing the limitations of even the most elaborate techniques, foresters have brought about a quiet revolution in fire policy. Most foresters now regard fire fighting as part of overall forest management rather than as a separate, crisis-oriented undertaking. This is an important distinction, for the forest-management approach often allows for natural burning in some situations; fire itself is considered to be one of the foresters' most useful tools.

By the early 20th Century, many lumbermen working in the American South realized that fire had a place in the management of the region's long-leaf pine forests. These tall evergreens, which have few branches and irregularly shaped crowns, combine with slash pine to provide not only timber but valuable foraging areas for livestock. After decades of practical experience, woodsmen concluded that longleaf pine forests require fire in their life cycle, to replenish the soil nutrients and to melt resins that encase seeds. By the 1930s, foresters also realized that controlled burning helped curb the brown spot needle blight, a disease that periodically ravaged the woodlands, and that a fire improved the nutrient value and palatability of the low-growing plants favored by grazing animals in such forests. Moreover, they observed that in the absence of fire, the highly flammable saw palmetto scrub flourished—and once this plant became well established the threat of very intense fires, sufficient to spread the flames to the crowns of the pines, increased.

Gradually, forest managers began to experiment with prescribed fire—deliberately setting fire to portions of the forest to achieve a variety of goals: preparing seedbeds, reducing the hazard of wildfire, controlling certain tree diseases and manipulating wildlife habitats. The practice has now spread from the South to most of the forests of the United States. Throughout the timberlands of the West, for example, prescribed burning has been used regularly to clean up slash after lumbering operations and to create seedbeds for reforestation efforts. But deliberately set blazes are not always practical as forest-management tools. In many woodlands, for example, traditional fire-suppression techniques have been used for so long that the forest floors have built up dangerous levels of flammable litter. The accumulation is so great in some areas that no one has figured out how to burn it off deliberately without causing a major, uncontrolled fire. This is particularly true of many of the Western ponderosa pine and Douglas fir forests.

Considerable research is under way to determine which techniques of prescribed burning work best in which kinds of forest. A number of foresters are concentrating their studies on chaparral, a forest-like type of vegetation common in Southern California. Wildfires in such woodlands often destroy homes and even whole neighborhoods, and they lead to such erosion problems as massive mud slides. Chaparral grows in places with a Mediterranean climate—mild, moist winters and hot, dry summers. This type of growth is characterized by such plants as hard-wooded conifers, evergreen oaks and thorny shrubs, which have extensive roots, dense, rigid branching, and small leaves that often contain a highly flammable resin.

In a way, the plant's flammability is an evolutionary development that promotes fire and encourages the growth of new generations of vegetation. Most chaparral plants grow so rapidly that a large number of their branches are dead and tinder-dry within about 25 years. When fire clears away these mature plants, they are almost immediately replaced by fast-growing descendants. Many chaparral shrubs have durable roots that regenerate the plants quickly after a fire and give them a head start on competing species; others depend upon fire to create a soil chemistry favorable for seed germination. Indeed, the chaparral's life cycle is so bound up with periodic fire that control measures have actually threatened the survival of 15 species.

Suppressing chaparral fires is increasingly expensive and not very effective. Forest managers are now seeking ways of using prescribed fire as a prevention device. Young chaparral stands, for example, do not burn readily, so the objective is to break up large stands of older trees into a mosaic of different ages, making it difficult for wildfire to spread. But fire suppression has already allowed many trees to age dangerously, increasing the chance that even prescribed burns will erupt into destructive wildfire.

Forestry workers and researchers take their ease as a fire rages through chaparral in Southern California. After bulldozing firebreaks around the area, the foresters set this fire to burn out deadwood, rejuvenate the scrub and reduce the chance of a later, catastrophic blaze.

The natural tendency of dry woodlands to erupt in flames was starkly demonstrated in Western Australia in 1983, when a series of wildfires devastated some 1.25 million acres. After several years of drought, a number of fires were touched off accidentally in different areas near Melbourne as dry summer winds swept down from the northern desert. Impelled by the seasonal winds, which often exceeded 50 miles per hour, the fires raced over parched grasslands and roared through dry eucalyptus forests. Some 5,000 fire fighters battled the blazes, but they could do little to suppress the flames. In places, years of prescribed burning had reduced the flammable litter on the forest floor; but much of the region had been deemed too densely populated for such controlled burning programs, and when the flames arrived, entire neighborhoods and even towns were swiftly consumed. When the fire was finally brought under control, at least 2,500 houses had been destroyed, 74 people had been killed and 2,000 injured.

However natural or inevitable such fires may be, a full-scale counterattack by fire fighters is always in order when lives and property are threatened. But if circumstances are not dire, foresters may experiment with a less energetic response. Since 1977 foresters in the United States have been considering their options carefully when a fire is not easily stopped and its potential for damage is low. Often, they will use a check list of questions designed to help determine their proper course. The first question is whether life or property is endangered: If the answer is yes, a vigorous attack is indicated. But if the answer is no, the foresters go to the next question: Will the weather make the fire worse? If not, they proceed to questions about fire behavior, boundaries and a variety of other factors. Given a certain set of conditions, a forest manager might use only minimal suppression methods—a few ground crews with hand tools, for example—rather than summon such elaborate resources as were thrown unsuccessfully against the Sundance Mountain fire.

And in certain areas of the United States, called Fire Management Areas, a fire that meets the criteria of a beneficial natural fire may be allowed to burn without interference. One such area is the Troy Ranger District—a 70,000-acre parcel on the Idaho-Montana border near Canada, not far from Sundance Mountain. Heavily forested and managed primarily for timber and big game, this sparsely populated area is sometimes allowed to burn unhindered in the spring or winter, when rains are likely to limit damage.

For all the benefits that some forest fires can bring, the sight of scorched, blackened woodland is troubling, as is the thought of forest managers watching while a wildfire burns. But from Sundance Mountain to southern Australia, mounting evidence suggests that at times the most effective strategy of all may be to do nothing, to let the flames proceed with the work they have been doing since the first forests appeared on earth. Ω

WEAPONS FOR A HOT WAR

The armies that take to the field against the world's forest fires have enlisted a broad spectrum of modern technology in their battles. But the objectives of fire fighters in the forest remain the classic ones of raising the alarm promptly, deploying needed resources quickly, and denying to the fire at least one of its vital requirements of oxygen, heat and fuel.

It takes time to move fire fighters and equipment to a remote forest site, and early detection of wildfire is a must. When thunderstorms threaten in the U.S. Northwest, for instance, electronic devices with a range of 250 miles scan the skies for the especially powerful lightning bolts that ignite thousands of fires every year. Infrared sensors aboard patrol planes probe the forest during dry seasons for ominous hot spots and, finding an established blaze, penetrate even dense smoke to pinpoint the location and shape of the fire front. When the data on the fire, plus information on terrain and weather forecasts, are analyzed by computer, managers can predict the fire's course and deploy their forces with maximum efficiency.

In remote forests, fire fighters known as smokejumpers may parachute into frontline positions to clear areas where helicopters can deposit heavy equipment such as bulldozers and water tankers. Aircraft are also used in more direct assaults, to drop water or chemicals on the blaze. Usually these measures are designed to slow the fire's advance until other forces can be brought into play. The battle that follows can be brutal. Barriers of clear land are bulldozed; earth is shoveled on embers; brush is hacked away. Even so, natural processes —a wind shift, for instance—are more likely to stop the fire than all the skill and energy mere humans can muster.

Launching an aerial assault on a forest fire in the American Northwest, a converted World War II bomber unleashes a cascade of slurry, a flame-retarding mix of clay, water and dye.

A helicopter scoops water from a reservoir to fight a nearby fire in New Zealand. A valve in the bottom of the specially designed bucket allows it to fill with water when it is dunked.

Perilously close to the turbulence generated
by a New Zealand blaze, a helicopter pilot opens
the valve in his bucket to douse the leading
edge of the fire with a 150-gallon load of water.

A smokejumper who has parachuted into position ahead of an advancing wildfire ignites a backfire that will be drawn toward the larger blaze by convection currents.

40

As smoke from an approaching blaze begins
to darken the sky, a smokejumper guides his
descent toward an opening in the dense
canopy of a remote forest in Alaska.

As sheets of flame roar toward them, a hard-pressed fire crew prepares to evacuate a pump truck that has brought 650 gallons of water to the battle against an Australian wildfire.

A bulldozer topples an already-smoldering tree in an attempt to scour a firebreak before a fire front arrives. If the break is too narrow, the blaze could leap over it and trap the crew.

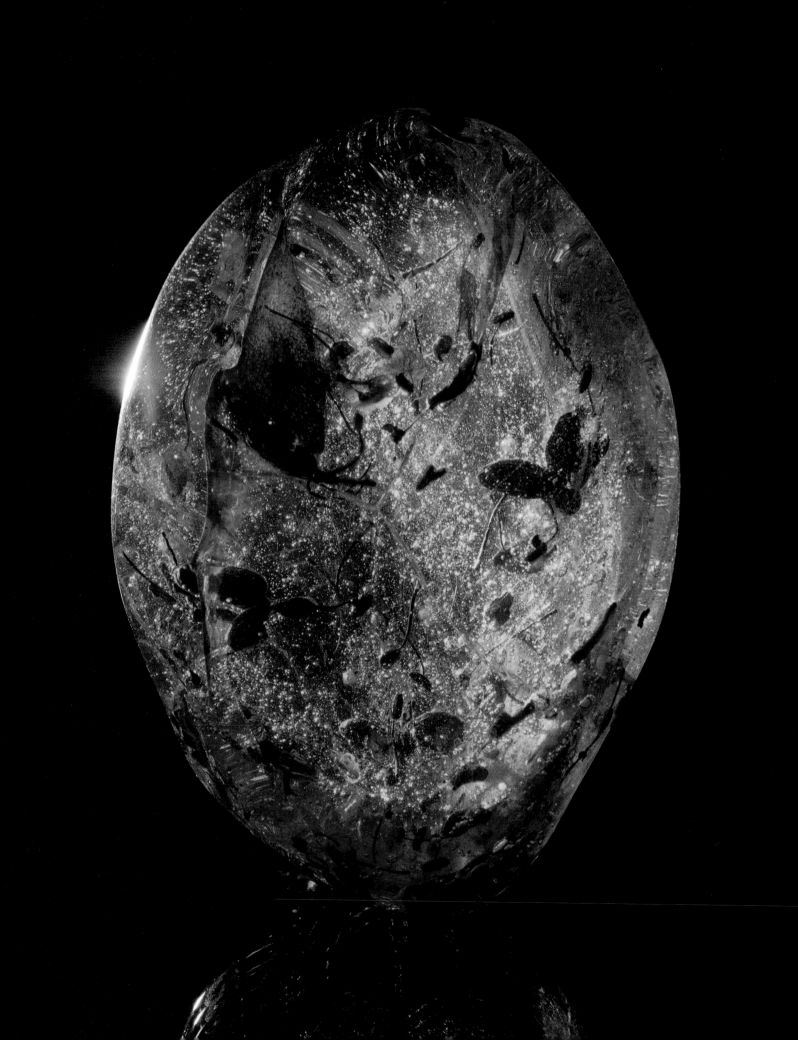

GREAT AGES OF PLANTS

A sudden downpour in the autumn of 1869 altered the usual quiet and bucolic course of life in the Catskill Mountains of eastern New York State. A stream that normally gurgled placidly down from the forested mountains suddenly surged over its banks and roared past the town of Gilboa, tearing out roadbeds and washing bridges away. For the little community, it was a disaster, calling for months of hard and expensive work to repair the damage. A few days later, townspeople inspecting the mangled creek bed came across a place where the rushing waters had excavated the banks down to a bed of sandstone, revealing a group of tree stumps that appeared to be made of stone.

Such fossils, found at many locations around the world, are of interest chiefly to a small group of specialists called paleobotanists, who read images of prehistoric stumps, stems and leaves to learn how, why and when forests and other forms of plant life came into being. The very fact of their preservation is fascinating in its own right. Plant fossils are frequently found embedded deeply in solid rock, bespeaking the slow procession of eons; but these relics of ancient vegetation are also the products of speed: The original plant materials had to be buried quickly, before they were destroyed by oxygen and by the microorganisms that feed on such tissues.

A site near the little town of Puryear, Tennessee, exemplifies one way the preservation can occur. Fifty million years ago a lagoon was situated there, and each year the surrounding trees and shrubs dropped their leaves into the water. This debris sank to the muddy bottom, where each year's accumulation of leaves was covered rapidly by a layer of silt built up as streams carried fine-grained soil into the lagoon. Pressed between the old and new silt layers, the leaves formed an impression in the muck that remained after the organic matter in the leaves had decayed. Later, the land was uplifted and the clay dried out, hardened and in time was transformed into sedimentary rock, preserving for all time the fossil images of the prehistoric leaves.

In most cases, the more rapidly the organic matter is buried, the more slowly it decomposes. Sometimes the results are spectacular. For example, while the lagoon was filling up in Puryear, a volcanic eruption in what is now Yellowstone National Park toppled thousands of trees in a huge and highly diverse forest, then smothered the area with layers of ash hundreds of feet deep. Rain water absorbed large amounts of silica from the ash, then percolated down through the layers and began to permeate the organic material of the buried forest. Inside the wood tissues, quartz crystals precipitated out of the mineral-rich water, providing a nearly perfect cast

A three-inch lump of amber from the Dominican Republic entombs flower parts from a tropical hardwood forest of 25 to 30 million years ago. A flow of resin engulfed the flowers, then was transformed to amber by physical and chemical changes operating over millions of years.

45

The fossil stump of an ancient tree is hoisted from the site of its discovery near Gilboa, New York, in 1921. The 350-million-year-old tree, shown below in a reconstruction by a paleobotanist, grew to a height of 40 feet in swampy coastal terrain.

of the structural details of the wood cells. As the trees were becoming fossilized belowground, a new forest took root in the nutritious volcanic soil above. It, too, would be buried by a volcanic eruption in time, as would its successors.

In the 1870s, while archeologist William Henry Holmes was surveying the Yellowstone region, he discovered an eroded cliffside where the stumpy quartz remains of 10 such forests were exposed to view. "The bleached trunks of the ancient forests stand out on the ledges like the columns of a ruined temple," he reported. Subsequent investigations at the site revealed that at least 17 other ancient forests had flourished and then fallen victim to volcanoes in Yellowstone, each one deriving nourishment from the ash that had destroyed the last.

The stumps that were uncovered near Gilboa, New York, in 1869 were formed in much the same way, possibly after the original trees had been covered by a mud slide. While their appearance was not nearly so striking as the layered remains at Yellowstone, they would play an important part in expanding scientists' knowledge of the earliest forests. The size, shape and proportions of the fossil trunks indicated that the trees had grown from

46

bulbous bases that must have been deeply embedded in the soil, since the small, straplike roots around the bases did not appear to be capable of supporting tall, freestanding trees. And the trees must have been sizable; judging from the four-foot diameter of one stump and the architecture preserved in the fossils, scientists estimated that they reached 40 feet in height. The trunks tapered gradually and most likely supported crowns of fernlike fronds.

When they dated the sandstone in which the fossils were found, the scientists concluded that the trees had lived some 350 million years ago, during the geological period called the Devonian. The age of the specimens was not particularly surprising; it had long been assumed that isolated clumps of trees and treelike plants had existed that far back in the past. But in 1897, some fossil stumps of the same age were uncovered about a mile north of the original discovery; in 1920, more relics were found nearly a mile and a quarter to the south; and during the next few years, several others turned up nearby. Until then, no one had imagined that forests existed in the inconceivably distant Devonian times, but the evidence was undeniable; a woodland covering hundreds of acres—the earliest known forest on the planet—had once blanketed the area.

With a little imagination it is possible to visualize the primeval land-scape. The ancient forest grew along a low, swampy shore laced with streams. The climate was warm and humid, and the sparse fronds filtered the sun only slightly, creating dappled shade on the sodden forest floor. Except for the murmur of the wind and the monotonous crash of waves on what was then the shore of a nearby sea, silence reigned. There were no birdsongs, not even the buzz of insects, because these higher forms of life had not yet evolved.

Only the earliest ancestors of a few crawling insects and spiders prowled the forest floor. In 1971, paleobotanists scouring an excavation site near Gilboa came across fossils of a centipede, a spider, an extinct form of mite and bits of a creature that may have been a forerunner of the silverfish. Some 365 million years old, the fossils were the oldest animal remains found in North America, and were probably among the first life forms fully adapted to life on dry land. The spider, about four hundredths of an inch long, resembled the familiar daddy longlegs found throughout that area today; the centipede was equipped with tiny fangs similar to the poisonous fangs of modern centipedes. These early predators probably fed upon tiny, soft-bodied forest creatures that left no fossils.

It had taken a long time to produce this forest. Like all living things, the trees of Gilboa were the result of tens of millions of years of evolution, an endless trial-and-error process in which genetic mutations occur, probably at random, and each new variant is tested by its environment. Most of the trials fail, and evolutionary history is littered with mutants that did not survive beyond a few generations. But others thrive and eventually give rise to even more successful progeny. Piecing together the history of these myriad natural experiments from the fragments of evidence that can be delved from the earth and inferred from observed plant behavior is scientific detective work at its most difficult. Thus, the discovery of a few pieces of fossil trees at Gilboa was of considerable significance, because it helped scientists establish approximately how long it had taken for the world's first forms of plant life to develop into widespread forests.

Life on earth began more than three billion years ago, probably in dark tidal pools or in the ocean depths. The surface of the earth was bombarded by ultraviolet rays from the sun, and only the protection of the water permitted the first bits of living matter that formed there to survive, sustaining themselves by breaking down and digesting inorganic compounds such as hydrogen sulfide and oxides of sulfur and iron. Eventually these prototypical life forms evolved into early forms of algae and bacteria, some of which were capable of making their own food by photosynthesis. This remarkable process uses the radiant energy of sunlight to transform carbon dioxide and water into sugars from which chemical energy is derived.

The heyday of these tiny food producers is known as the age of algae—the first of the four great ages of plants. It lasted for about 2.5 billion years, roughly half the life of the earth itself, and during this time the microscopic organisms prepared the way for their successors. As they propagated, spreading in billions through the primeval oceans and photosynthesizing their minute stores of nutrients, they continuously created, as a by-product, tiny increments of oxygen. Some of this was consumed by other primitive organisms that had developed respiration, some was chemically trapped in oxides of various metals, and a critical fraction found its way into the atmosphere, which had been chiefly composed of methane and carbon dioxide earlier in the planet's history.

When free oxygen in the atmosphere is struck by ultraviolet rays, it may rearrange itself into a three-atom form known as ozone, which is capable of blocking subsequent ultraviolet rays. Since ozone is created at the highest levels of accumulated oxygen, and since it tends to protect the oxygen below, an ozone layer persists at an altitude of 20 to 30 miles. After the age of algae had lasted about two billion years, enough ozone had accumulated to significantly reduce the amount of deadly radiation reaching the earth's surface. Life was still not tenable on the land, but in the protective oceans, evolutionary experiment and change accelerated: The water began to teem with a variety of life, including multicellular animals such as sponges, corals and jellyfish. Algae became more complex and developed into long filaments and flat blades of seaweed. As plants multiplied, photosynthesis increased until, about 400 million years ago, oxygen made up about 2 per cent of the atmosphere—one tenth its current level. Now, enough ultraviolet light was being blocked so that life outside the nurturing oceans became possible. The land masses of the earth were about to be invaded by an army of plant life.

No one knows for sure how the plants' move to dry land was achieved. But scientists speculate that some types of green algae growing at the margins of streams and tidal pools evolved into branched forms that could survive in the open air during brief periods of low water—even without leaves to collect the energy of the sun. Two basic features would have been essential to the survival of the first terrestrial life: a waxy covering called a cuticle, to help the plant retain moisture, and a vascular system—a collection of tubes that could carry water up from the ground and carry food, manufactured by photosynthesis, down from the green parts to the base of the plant. Chemical analyses of fossils indicate that the cell walls of some prehistoric algae contained cellulose similar to that found in today's land plants, and that these ancient plants stored food as starch, just as most modern plants do.

The petrified remains of trees that grew 200 million years ago litter the now-treeless landscape of Petrified Forest National Park, Arizona. During its long burial, the wood gradually absorbed mineral deposits that preserved much of its structure, including the pattern of annual growth rings.

48

Bared by the erosion of volcanic ash, the petrified remains of an ancient forest stand amid living trees in Yellowstone National Park *(above)*. Some 50 million years ago, 27 successive forests were buried on the site by ash from a series of volcanic eruptions *(diagram, left)* that continued for 20,000 years.

The first such land plant to appear in the fossil record is Cooksonia, found in rock strata that date back some 400 million years. Initially identified in Wales in 1937, Cooksonia was a slender, leafless growth that branched upward in a symmetrically forked pattern to a height of about two inches. This pioneer had tiny, globular spore-producing elements, called sporangia, on the tips of its branches. Spores were a new and vital asset to the evolution of plants on land. More primitive organisms such as bacteria and single-celled algae had relied on simple cell division to reproduce themselves, a method that severely restricted their distribution on land. But with the advent of spores, which were about the size of fine dust particles and had a waterproof covering that kept them from drying out as they floated on the wind, widespread dispersal became possible.

Cooksonia was the first of a family of plants known as the rhyniophytes. Scientists do not know whether this family was the progenitor of all other land plants, one of many progenitors or just an evolutionary dead end. But they do know that its appearance on land coincided with the beginning of the second great era of growing things—the age of the lower vascular plants. That era began about 395 million years ago, just before the start of the Devonian period, and was characterized by spectacular evolutionary progress.

The surge was slow in getting under way, however. The fossil record indicates that a few million years passed before a distinctly different type of plant joined Cooksonia and its relatives on the Devonian landscape. Called the zosterophyllophytes, these newcomers were much larger than the rhyniophytes, and their sporangia were arranged along the sides of the stems instead of at the tips. Though a seemingly minor modification, this design dramatically increased the number of sporangia, improving the plants' chances for survival by allowing more spore production.

Evolution dawdled for another five million years or so. Then, in the space of about 16 million years, many different types of plants with larger stems appeared. Among them was a family known as the psilophytes, which had a single stem, or axis, and smaller lateral branches (Cooksonia branched only by equal divisions of the stem). Over time, some of the psilophytes developed a new kind of woody tissue that increased both the strength of their stems and their ability to transport water upward. With the aid of this tissue, some plants grew taller and larger, and the earliest form of tree emerged.

This period also saw the appearance of progymnosperms, a variety of tall plants with frondlike branches. The unique asset of the progymnosperms—which are thought to be the ancestors of present-day gymnosperms, including such trees as pines, firs and redwoods—was an unusually large and strong stem. By now, so many low-growing plants had spread across the land that the competition for sunlight had become a factor in survival, and a woody stem offered an unbeatable height advantage. Moreover, the additional layers of wood increased the capacity of the plant's vascular system, which in turn made further growth possible; some of the progymnosperms grew as high as 120 feet.

The progymnosperms were followed by other treelike plants whose horizontal branches grew in a line that wound up the main stem in a pattern somewhat like the steps of a spiral staircase. Over time, some of the small lateral twigs on the branches became webbed; in one plant called Archaeop-

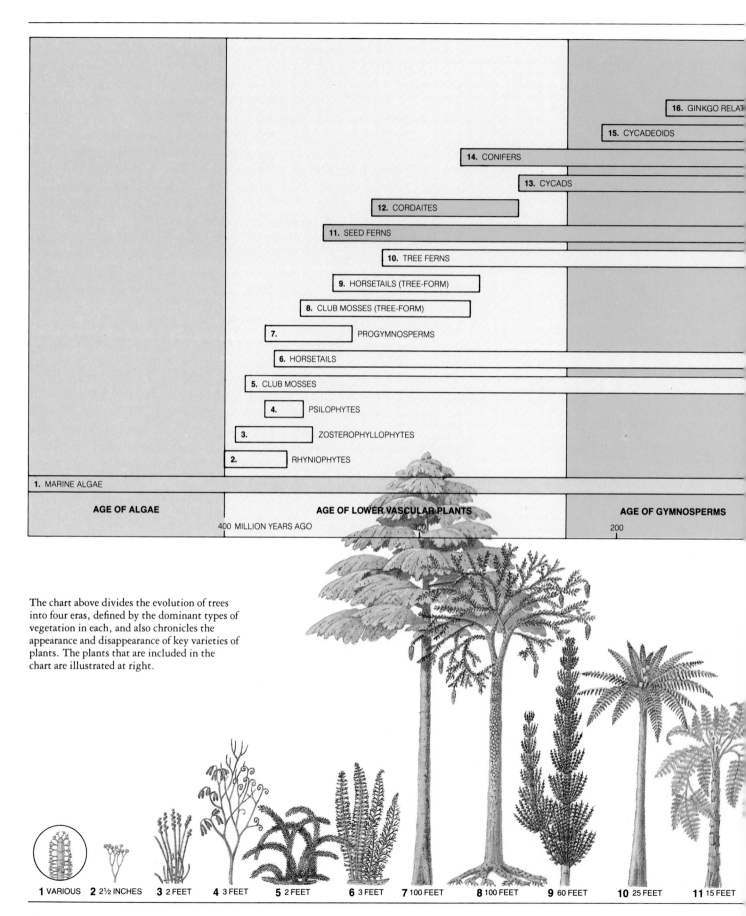

16. GINKGO RELAT

15. CYCADEOIDS

14. CONIFERS

13. CYCADS

12. CORDAITES

11. SEED FERNS

10. TREE FERNS

9. HORSETAILS (TREE-FORM)

8. CLUB MOSSES (TREE-FORM)

7. PROGYMNOSPERMS

6. HORSETAILS

5. CLUB MOSSES

4. PSILOPHYTES

3. ZOSTEROPHYLLOPHYTES

2. RHYNIOPHYTES

1. MARINE ALGAE

AGE OF ALGAE **AGE OF LOWER VASCULAR PLANTS** **AGE OF GYMNOSPERMS**

400 MILLION YEARS AGO   300   200

The chart above divides the evolution of trees into four eras, defined by the dominant types of vegetation in each, and also chronicles the appearance and disappearance of key varieties of plants. The plants that are included in the chart are illustrated at right.

1 VARIOUS **2** 2½ INCHES **3** 2 FEET **4** 3 FEET **5** 2 FEET **6** 3 FEET **7** 100 FEET **8** 100 FEET **9** 60 FEET **10** 25 FEET **11** 15 FEET

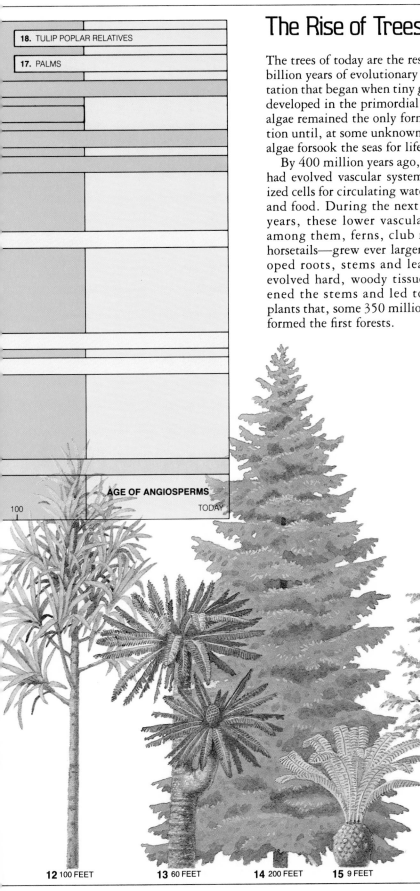

AGE OF ANGIOSPERMS

100

TODAY

The Rise of Trees

The trees of today are the result of three billion years of evolutionary experimentation that began when tiny green plants developed in the primordial seas. These algae remained the only form of vegetation until, at some unknown date, a few algae forsook the seas for life on land.

By 400 million years ago, land plants had evolved vascular systems—specialized cells for circulating water, minerals and food. During the next 50 million years, these lower vascular plants—among them, ferns, club mosses and horsetails—grew ever larger and developed roots, stems and leaves. Some evolved hard, woody tissue that stiffened the stems and led to the giant plants that, some 350 million years ago, formed the first forests.

But the reproductive system of lower vascular plants relies on spores and structures that are fertile only in a moist environment. The gymnosperms, the next great wave of vegetation to dominate forests, triumphed because they had seeds. Sheathed in a protective coating and packed with nutrients for the embryo, a seed can endure harsh, dry conditions before germinating.

The latest phase in the development of forests began when flowering trees, or angiosperms, appeared. Their methods of reproduction are far more efficient than those of earlier flora. While gymnosperms rely on the wind to disperse pollen, many flowering plants attract nectar-seeking insects and birds that unwittingly aid in pollination.

12 100 FEET   **13** 60 FEET   **14** 200 FEET   **15** 9 FEET   **16** 80 FEET   **17** 130 FEET   **18** 190 FEET

teris, they appeared as small bladelike appendages—the first recognizable leaves. With their increased surface area, leaves provided an enormous advantage to organisms that depended on collecting solar energy to fuel the vital process of photosynthesis. Archaeopteris and its near relatives, along with some tree-sized club mosses and fern ancestors, made up the ancient forest uncovered in Gilboa, New York.

Meanwhile, spores had also been evolving. On the earliest land plants, the sporangia at the tips of the stems contained only one kind of spore, though each spore had the potential to generate either male or female plants. In time, however, the spores themselves came to be specialized, each developing in its own sporangium, and the male spores tending to be smaller than the female. Over many generations, the female spores approached the size of specks of pepper, and the female sporangium contained fewer and fewer of the larger spores. The tiny male spores, meanwhile, remained so numerous that the probability was still high that one of them would fertilize a female. The next evolutionary step was taken when the sporangium holding the female spores became enclosed in a thin skin, or integument, to form a rudimentary seed. No one knows exactly how this occurred, but scientists are agreed that seeds appeared about 50 million years after vascular plants evolved. The world's most venerable seed fossils—discovered in 1981 in Randolph County, West Virginia—are 350 million years old.

By about 345 million years ago, the fundamental character of the earth's vegetation had been determined. Not only had plant life entrenched itself ashore, but it had adjusted to all but the most forbidding terrestrial wastelands. More and more plants developed the woody architecture that guaranteed a secure place in the sun, and groves of these early trees spread out over the landscape, becoming so large and numerous that they not only survived in their environment, they influenced it significantly. At this important evolutionary moment, now indistinguishable in the distant millennia, the first forests—extensive tracts in which the life cycles of trees and other vegetation are closely intertwined—came into being.

During the next 65 million years or so, club mosses and horsetails flourished. Many became treelike and soared more than 100 feet above the sodden and crowded terrain. Some remained herbaceous (lacking woody stems) and filled in the extensive swampy forests where newer plants, such as spore-producing true ferns, were also emerging. Gymnosperms were present, too—ferns that grew 25 feet tall and had complex seeds, and conifers with large trunks, needle-like leaves, and cones.

Animals added another dimension to the forest environment. Many types of insects evolved, feeding on plant matter and on one another. The forest floor was alive with huge cockroaches, some more than six inches long, and giant dragonflies with wingspans of about two feet droned through the air. Amphibians plied the murky waters, setting the stage for the higher animals' migration to dry land. Most were small, similar to salamanders, although fearsome razor-toothed predators as big as today's alligators also inhabited the swamps and streams.

If the future was bright for animals, the present was positively refulgent for plants. They grew in such abundance that their fossil remains would create one of the most important resources of the modern world—coal.

When trees die and fall into water, as they did by the millions into the swamps and marshes of 300 million years ago, bacteria digest the leaves and

Fossil Forests in the Making

The geologic processes that turn once-living material into fossils continue today, overtaking forests that in the far-distant future may be unearthed and studied for clues to their time.

Most fallen trees soon vanish, dismantled by insects, bacteria, fungi and chemical breakdown. But a few trees are protected from disintegration by a quick burial and become candidates for fossilization. Most of these fall into swamps, riverbeds and tidal mud flats, where they are quickly blanketed by sediments. Others may be entombed by volcanic eruptions or by shifting sand dunes. Occasionally, a tree topples into a hot spring, where it is soon encased by an armor of mineral deposits, or into the enveloping ooze of a tar seep.

If the material surrounding a buried tree eventually hardens into rock, a fossil imprint of the tree may endure long after the wood itself has turned to dust. If seeping groundwater infiltrates the buried wood with mineral deposits that assume the shape and texture of its tissue, the petrified substance of the tree may be preserved indefinitely. The pressure of deep burial may transform the wood to carbon—the coal deposit of tomorrow. But the most stunning fossils of the future may emerge from tar seeps, where the asphalt so effectively excludes oxygen and other agents of decay that an entire tree may be disgorged, scarcely altered, millions of years after it falls.

A denuded forest of conifers near the Oregon coast juts from the shifting sands that choked the trees. If the sand buries the trees and is later transformed into rock by geologic change, the dead forest may one day be found in the form of fossils embedded in sandstone.

Algae-encrusted trees drowned by rising sea level sprawl on mud flats on the coast of England. The accumulating sediment may eventually preserve the trees as fossils.

Empty stone husks commemorate a forest that was caught in a 1790 volcanic eruption on Hawaii. A flood of lava coated the trees, then subsided to leave these fossil molds of solid rock.

In Yellowstone National Park, Wyoming, dead trees litter the mineral-rich water of a hot spring that poisoned them decades before. Accumulating mineral deposits may eventually encrust or even petrify the logs.

A skeletal forest of fir trees gives way to marsh grasses on the Notsuke Peninsula of Japan, where a 1954 typhoon transformed tracts of forest into salt marsh and poisoned the trees. High waves regularly wash across the narrow peninsula, burying fallen trees in sand.

A natural lake of tar on the island of Trinidad gradually engulfs a log. The tar poisons microorganisms and in effect embalms the wood, preserving it indefinitely.

Leaves and fruit from an alder tree are shown being buried by river silt *(left)*. If the sediment continues to accumulate and eventually consolidates to form rock, a fossil impression—much like the 30,000-year-old imprint of an elm leaf shown above—may be preserved.

other fleshy parts first and then, less quickly, the wood. But this decomposition can be carried only so far: Most bacteria need oxygen, and the water limits the amount of oxygen available to those at work on the fallen trees. Without sustained bacterial action, the dead vegetation does not decompose entirely into gases and water-soluble compounds but becomes a soft black muck called peat. Once dried, peat will burn relatively well, because its carbon content is much higher than was that of the original vegetation. This is not because carbon has been added, but because other components such as hydrogen and oxygen have been reduced or released as gases by the bacterial action and squeezed out by the weight of sediments accumulating on top of the peat.

In order for coal to form from peat, the peat bog must be completely covered with water. Then, as more sediments drain into the area, layers of sand and mud eventually build up on top of the peat. The added pressure further compacts the material, squeezing out so much hydrogen and oxygen in the form of gaseous compounds that the peat hardens into lignite, or brown coal—almost 70 per cent carbon, compared with the 60 per cent carbon content of peat. As even more rock accumulates over the lignite, increased heat and pressure continue to force out other volatile compounds, until the lignite becomes bituminous coal, which has a carbon content of more than 80 per cent. And if the bituminous coal is in turn subjected to the tremendous heat and pressure generated by tectonic movement in the earth's crust, such as mountain building, the coal is further purified into anthracite, which is 95 per cent carbon. Anthracite, the most desirable of coals because it burns best and generates the fewest impurities, is usually found deep in the earth, frequently in the vicinity of mountain ranges.

While most of the world's largest coal beds contain bituminous coal that was laid down in the steamy age of lower vascular plants, coal has been forming continually ever since, wherever plant decay is incomplete. Huge lignite deposits were created in Europe just 50 million years ago, when dense forests flourished there in a climate that was somewhat warmer than it is today. The geologic evidence shows that such warm periods, often lasting millions of years, have occurred many times since then, nurturing lush forests even inside the Arctic Circle. Fossils found in coal beds near Anchorage, Alaska, reveal that palm trees grew there just 30 million years ago, when the land area had already moved into its present latitude. At about the same time, extensive forests blanketed Greenland, which was also in its current place, and eventually created enough organic residue to allow coal beds to form. (Steamships plying the Atlantic in the 19th Century, when Greenland was again virtually entombed by mile-thick sheets of ice, routinely put in there to refuel their coal-fired boilers with the remains of ancient tropical forests.) But in none of the more recent coal-making periods has the sheer volume of vegetation produced in the age of the lower vascular plants been surpassed.

The climatic changes that brought an end to the great coal-producing period some 225 million years ago also triggered the next major step in forest evolution. Although the shifts in humidity and temperature were gradual, the resulting alterations in the length and severity of the seasons had profound effects. Over a period of some 35 million years, the giant club mosses and horsetails began to die out, leaving behind only the small herbaceous versions that inhabit the planet today. As the world's climate became drier, the age of the spore-producing vascular plants, with their dependence on water, gave way to the age of the gymnosperms and their durable seeds.

Throughout the next 150 million years—the time of the dinosaurs—

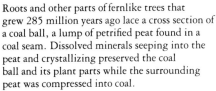

Roots and other parts of fernlike trees that grew 285 million years ago lace a cross section of a coal ball, a lump of petrified peat found in a coal seam. Dissolved minerals seeping into the peat and crystallizing preserved the coal ball and its plant parts while the surrounding peat was compressed into coal.

ROOTS

ROOTS

ROOTS

ROOTS

STEM   LEAF BASE

gymnosperms dominated the forests of the world. Two that emerged then have descended virtually unchanged to the present: the cycads, with thick stubby trunks surmounted by large palmlike leaves; and the ginkgos, with small, fan-shaped leaves. As in earlier times, the gymnosperms shared their reign with ferns, which now appeared in diverse forms ranging from 30-foot-tall trees to small, low-growing vines. Such diversification was assured because, by 200 million years ago, the planet's land masses were drifting apart. The lands that once had formed a single huge continent began to move toward their present positions on the globe, carrying different species in different directions. A great rift opened up between the African and South American land masses some 100 million years ago; by the time the dinosaurs died out some 35 million years later, it had widened to oceanic size. Meanwhile, the animal and plant populations on either side evolved along different courses.

Just before the dinosaurs vanished, another great revolution took place in the plant kingdom. This was the arrival of the rugged and versatile flowering plants called angiosperms—an event that marked the beginning of the fourth great age of plants. When Charles Darwin contemplated the intricate and cryptic fossil record of the first flowering plants more than a century ago, he pronounced the subject an "abominable mystery." And the mystery remains to this day. Few fossils of delicate flowers have survived, but a sudden abundance of fossilized wood, leaves and pollen, appearing in the fossil record about 120 million years ago, proves that angiosperms were by then widespread: The remains of so many angiosperms indicate a long evolution of flowering plants, perhaps beginning back beyond the age of the dinosaurs. Some scientists have suggested no evidence of these earlier plants survives because angiosperms evolved in drier highland areas, where wind and erosion interfere with fossil formation. It is also possible that all of the angiosperm traits combined into a form so effective that it triumphed over the less versatile gymnosperms with unprecedented speed.

The name angiosperm, taken from the Latin, means "covered seed." While the gymnosperms expose their ovules—the female organs of the reproductive process—to the air (as for example on the leaflike scales of a pine cone) the angiosperms enclose their ovules at the bases of the flowers, lodged within elements called ovaries. Also, the gymnosperms store food in the female reproductive organs before fertilization takes place, and since fertilization is never a sure thing, the stored energy is sometimes wasted. The angiosperms have a more sophisticated system: They store food in the female organ only after the egg has been fertilized.

Typically, in both gymnosperms and angiosperms, two male sperms penetrate to the ovule, but in gymnosperms, one fertilizes the egg, and the other degenerates. However, in the flowering angiosperms, both sperms perform vital functions: One fertilizes the egg, the other fuses with a special cell nucleus at the center of the embryo sac. While the fertilized egg develops into the seed—the embryo of the new plant—the other sperm and nucleus become what is known as an endosperm, the food supply for the embryo. The tissue surrounding the ovule then develops into a fruit, which protects the seeds from the weather and attracts animals that transport the seeds in their digestive tracts.

Among other evolutionary improvements, the angiosperms developed broad, net-veined leaves that allow the plants to make food more efficiently by photosynthesis. They also evolved large tubes in the xylem, the tissue that conducts water to all parts of the plant. These tubes allow water to flow in greater quantities than it does in the finely structured wood of the gymnosperms.

Almost as if attempting to hedge their evolutionary bets, the angiosperms developed along two distinctly different lines, the monocotyledons and dicotyledons, which even botanists find easier to call monocots and dicots. Both have leaf structures, called seed leaves, inside their seed cases; monocots have one seed leaf, dicots two. With the ability of the monocots to flourish in areas too dry for dicots, and the tolerance of dicots for shade that would stop the growth of a monocot, the effect of the diversity was to greatly expand the total range of the angiosperms.

There are other differences as well. Monocot flower parts grow in groups of three; dicot flower parts, such as petals, occur in groups of four or five. The veins in a monocot leaf are generally parallel, as in grasses, running along the length of the leaf, while dicots have webbed or netlike veins. Palm trees are monocots, but most other flowering trees are dicots.

The fossil record seems to indicate that monocots evolved later than dicots, but the evidence is not definitive. Scientists do know that the angiosperms proliferated at a remarkable rate, in a worldwide explosion of herbs, shrubs and, eventually, trees. One thing that enabled the angiosperms to spread so far and so quickly was the help that they received from animals, insects and birds. The wind had been the primary carrier of pollen, but about 100 million years ago the creatures of the forest, attracted to the sweet nectar of the flowers, started to play a much bigger role in plant development. Indeed, it is likely that flowering plants and certain insects and birds evolved in a kind of conjoined waltz through time. It is also possible that the arrival of the angiosperms made a happy niche for a new breed of shorter and squatter dinosaurs—perhaps the distant forerunners of some mammals—adapted to browsing on the shrubby and herbaceous early versions of these plants.

The efficacy of the angiosperm seeds is beyond doubt. Seeds encased in several protective layers of the fruit were far more resistant to changes in climate than were spores and unprotected seeds, and they were also more portable. When midocean volcanic islands, such as Hawaii and Iceland, rose steaming from the ocean floor miles from the continental land masses, they were absolutely sterile, but in the space of just a few years, angiosperms colonized them. Some monocot seeds, including coconuts, floated to these new-made lands and washed ashore onto nutrient-rich ash beaches; smaller dicot seeds were carried by birds, either attached to the feathers with little barbs or in the digestive tracts.

Gymnosperm seeds, on the other hand, have no covering and are more likely to dry out; in addition, they are often held in heavy, woody cones, so neither the birds nor the wind can carry them very far. Pine seeds have been transported by such natural means only a few hundred miles—for example, from the Pacific island of Guadalupe to Mexico. But flowering plants have reached every volcanic island, no matter how far from the nearest source of angiosperms.

Within a few million years of their debut on the planet, the flowering plants began evolving into trees, and soon they challenged the gymnosperms for hegemony of the forests. About 60 million years ago, oak, syca-

Survivors of a Vegetative Revolution

About 280 million years ago, seed-producing trees were taking the place of spore-bearing horsetails, club mosses and other primitive plants that had dominated the forests of the world until then. Their descendants, the modern conifers such as pines and firs, are common throughout the world. And a few of the pioneering tree varieties themselves survive, little changed from the days when they shared the earth with dinosaurs.

Three of these relicts are shown here, with their once-revolutionary means of reproduction. The graceful ginkgo tree *(top right)*, whose ancestors flourished worldwide 150 million years ago, at one time survived only in China, where it was cultivated in Buddhist temple gardens. The palmlike cycads *(bottom right)* have also declined. Cycads lived on nearly every continent 130 to 190 million years ago but now grow only in scattered tropical and subtropical locations and in hothouse gardens.

But the araucarias *(below)*, a family of primitive conifers, still forest large areas of South America, eastern Australia and New Zealand. And the araucaria forests of 200 million years ago left extensive petrified-wood deposits in both hemispheres. Like the other relict trees, araucarias are popular ornamentals; one species is the familiar Norfolk Island pine.

Ginkgos, cycads and araucarias are gymnosperms—seed-bearing trees that lack flowers and must depend on the wind to waft pollen from the male cones to fertilize the female cones. Their reproductive method, primitive by the standards of some of today's flowering trees, was the leading edge of progress in ancient swamp forests.

A monkey puzzle tree, a species of araucaria, lofts its branches above a mountainside in Chile. A cone, up to 8 inches in diameter *(inset)*, sheds winged seeds from a central axis.

Small fan-shaped leaves clothe the limbs of a ginkgo tree, a species that is practically extinct in the wild but a common planting along city streets. Its seeds *(inset)* have fleshy coatings that smell like rancid butter when fully ripe.

Palmlike fronds rise from the squat trunk of a cycad. This species of cycad develops seed-bearing cones weighing up to 90 pounds; other cycads bear open clusters of seeds *(inset)* that turn yellow as they mature.

more, walnut and fig had begun to supplant the outdated tree ferns, just as mammals, which had lurked about under the feet of the dinosaurs for many millennia, began to take over territory where reptiles had long held sway. At the same time, the movement of the continents was transforming the earth's surface, creating vastly different environmental conditions between the Poles and the Equator. The gymnosperms, not very tolerant of the shade created by the broad-leaved angiosperms, were relegated chiefly to colder climates and higher altitudes. Ferns, edged out of the most fertile lowlands, became smaller as they adapted to shadier, wetter areas—where they proliferate to this day.

Each of the four major stages of plant evolution represents a triumph of adaptation to climatic change, and once a new course was set, the survivors invariably made spectacular gains in their time. Of course, thousands of species perished when a new age was ushered in, but many of the outmoded species hung on, providing an important living link to the past. The miraculous beginning, the age of algae, is still in progress in the oceans and seas, and algae remain the first link in the food chain that supports all life on earth. After the lower vascular plants achieved the unprecedented status of true forests, they were overtaken by the seed-bearing gymnosperms; but the lower vascular plants survive in herbaceous forms that are well suited to limited environments. Even the gymnosperms, for all their durable wood trunks and branches, could not hold their own against the flowering plants. Although the coniferous gymnosperms still dominate the vast forestlands of the north, the present is clearly the age of prolific and versatile angiosperms, those stalwart flowering plants that range from the lowly buttercup to the towering oak. Ω

A saddle-back tortoise browses on the low branches of a young tree in the Galápagos Islands. In one of the most unusual adaptations to forest living, the tortoise has evolved a long neck and arched shell that enable it to reach leaves as much as five feet off the ground.

THE ANCESTRY OF FORESTS

Nothing remains of ancient forests but traceries in rock and a few plant parts preserved by quirks of geology. But this fossil record, supplemented by informed conjecture, has enabled scientists to reconstruct many of the key plants that lived during the middle and late Devonian period, 370 to 345 million years ago, when plants first attained treelike stature. An artist's composite of the reconstructions yields a hypothetical image of the world's first forest.

The geography of the era helped create an environment that was ideal for the lush growth of primitive plants: Large portions of the earth's land masses lay in the tropics, washed by warm, shallow seas. Along the shores towered plants with many of the basic features of modern trees—stout roots; massive, woody trunks rising up to 120 feet; and many-branched crowns.

But these primitive trees, flourishing long before the first large animals appeared on land, resembled their present-day counterparts only in barest outline; the conifers and flowering trees of today would not evolve for tens of millions of years. Instead, nature had improvised this dawn forest from some of the humblest of plants: enormous relatives of the spore-bearing, moisture-loving club mosses, ferns and horsetails that carpet low, shady spots on the floor of modern forests. Unaffected by seasonal change in the unvarying warm climate, unenlivened by the riot of animal life sustained by the seeds, fruit and flowers of modern trees, the primeval swamp forest was a silent, monotonous place, given over to the single activity of vegetative growth.

Gaunt, scaly relatives of modern club mosses *(left foreground)*, a tall, tapering ancestor of the horsetails *(left of center)*, and fernlike trees *(right)* dominate the swampy forest landscape of about 350 million years ago.

Advent of the Seed-Bearers

By about 280 million years ago, climatic and geologic processes left much of the earth drier and more mountainous than it had been before. The stresses of environmental change hastened plant evolution, and by 230 million years ago, a new kind of forest cloaked the land.

This recognizable ancestor of today's forests was shaped by a great evolutionary advance—the seed. The abundant water required to nurture the reproductive process of earlier vegetation restricted the horsetails, club mosses and fernlike plants of the earliest forests to swamps and shorelines. Because seeds can survive harsh conditions before germinating, seed-bearing trees colonized the drier ground and uplands that had replaced much of the primeval swampland. The domain of the giant, water-loving plants of the swamps was reduced to isolated patches of low ground.

Many of the trees in this ancestral forest were early representatives of the conifers—the group of trees that today dominates the world's evergreen forests. A few of the early seed-bearing species survive today almost unaltered, but others left no progeny. Seed-bearing ferns and urn-shaped plants with seed cones and crowns of fronds were to vanish tens of millions of years later during a new wave of evolutionary improvement—the emergence of flowering trees.

A forest of perhaps 200 million years ago spreads across lowlands and up a range of hills. Dinosaurs were just beginning their reign as the largest land animals, and many tree types found in modern forests had already evolved.

THE ANATOMY OF TREES

The 16th Century Belgian physician and theologian Jean Baptista van Helmont was a consistent enemy of conventional wisdom; he referred to traditional teachings in science and philosophy as "poor senseless prattle" and "dung." Needless to say, he was constantly at odds with the establishment of his day. According to one of his biographers, "pessimism, scepticism and criticism are the outstanding keynotes of all of van Helmont's works and researches."

Scion of a noble family, van Helmont made much of his refusal to accept money for practicing either of his principal professions, proclaiming that he refused to "live on the sins and miseries of the people." Yet despite his caustic tongue and heightened sense of importance, his contributions to science were far from being exclusively negative. He was, for instance, the first to determine that air is not a single substance but a mixture of gases; in fact, he is thought to have invented the word "gas."

In 1630, van Helmont turned his attention to trees. It had been generally accepted for at least two thousand years that trees drew their nourishment from the soil in which they were rooted, and questioning of the canon was handled simply by citing the revered Greek naturalist, Aristotle. It was precisely such close-mindedness that van Helmont loved to attack, and he managed to demolish conventional wisdom again in this case. But he needed extraordinary patience to do so. First he planted a carefully weighed five-pound willow sapling in a pot containing exactly 200 pounds of earth. He watered the plant regularly but added nothing else to the soil. Five years later, he uprooted the willow and carefully removed and collected all the soil. The tree then weighed 169 pounds, but the ground weighed only two ounces less than its original 200 pounds.

Van Helmont concluded correctly that the tree's food did not come from the soil. But he also concluded incorrectly that the weight gain was a result of the water added. Only after many years of painstaking study would researchers learn that trees nourish themselves by means of a complex chain of chemical reactions and physical processes.

The intricacy and delicacy of these processes is embodied, paradoxically, in one of the sturdiest of all materials—wood. Pound for pound it is stronger than steel; yet, as a casual glance at any sawed-off tree stump reveals, this utilitarian substance has a subtle structure. Two distinctly different types of material are immediately obvious; the rough outer skin of bark—which can range in thickness from less than a quarter of an inch in birch trees to as much as 24 inches in giant sequoias—and the wood itself.

A cloud of pollen falls from two male reproductive clusters, called catkins, on a birch tree; some of the grains, dispersed by the wind, will land on female flowers and pollinate them. Species that depend on the wind for pollination grow in dense stands, thus increasing the likelihood that fertilization will occur.

A closer visual inspection quickly reveals two subdivisions in each case. The corky outer layer of the bark, which consists of dead cells, grades imperceptibly into an inner, living layer of bark called the phloem. The wood itself consists of the light-colored sapwood, found just inside the bark, and the darker heartwood—particularly valued for commercial purposes because of its color, relative hardness and strength—found at the center of the stump.

What the naked eye cannot easily perceive, however, is the further, unimaginably complex specialization of cells required to carry on the living tree's vital processes of circulation and growth. A razor-thin band of material is responsible for these functions. Just inside the phloem lies a one-cell-thick layer—the vascular cambium—made up of cells that are capable of reproducing themselves and adding to the girth of the tree. During the growing season, the cells divide at a feverish pace, creating new tissue both inside and outside the vascular cambium.

The cells produced on the outside of the cambium become part of the phloem, forming a narrow sleeve that encases the trunk, all the branches and the major roots. The function of the phloem cells is to conduct nutrients manufactured in the leaves down to the roots; if the trunk's phloem is severed, the leaves may remain green for a while, but in time the roots starve and the tree dies. A portion of the phloem cells die each year and become part of the outer bark, which eventually sloughs off the tree in a process that is highly visible in the shaggy bark of the hickory and the delicate peels of bark that ring a birch.

The majority of the cells generated by the cambium accumulate on the inside of the layer as xylem and account for most of the increase in the tree's girth. In most temperate-zone trees, girth, which is customarily measured at a height of about five feet, increases at a rate of about one inch per year. For example, an oak tree with a trunk about eight feet in circumference at chest height is probably about 100 years old. There are some notable exceptions, however: Douglas firs and tulip poplars may add as much as three inches of girth in a good year, and Scots pines and horse chestnuts typically increase at a rate of less than an inch per year.

Xylem accumulates in two essentially different forms, generally known as softwood and hardwood. Only with the aid of a microscope can the cell structures that account for the distinction be perceived. The softwood of conifers, such as pines, consists of a honeycomb of cigar-shaped hollow cells that have several small pits on their sides. Called tracheids, these cells carry water and dissolved minerals from the tips of the roots all the way up to the needles. The water rises along a tortuous path: As one tracheid fills, the water percolates out through the side openings in the cell wall, through pits of adjacent tracheids, then upward and sideways again and again until it finally reaches the needles.

Hardwoods, such as oak, maple and hickory, have cells that permit a more direct flow of water and mineral nutrients. Hardwoods are characterized by cylindrical cells that form atop each other somewhat like sections of pipe. After they are joined, the tops and bottoms of adjacent cells dissolve to form continuous vessels that provide a direct route for transporting water and nutrients. The vessels occur in various sizes; oak vessels, for example, may have the diameter of a common straight pin, whereas those of maples and birches are usually only one sixth that size. Hardwood vessels alone do not have the structural strength of the more rugged tracheids, but they are

The roots of a fig tree form a woody tangle on the stone face of an ancient temple at Angkor, Kampuchea. Aerial roots are common in the tropics, where collections of humus and moisture in the forest canopy permit seeds to germinate above the ground and survive until their roots can reach the soil.

surrounded by long, thin fibers that provide support. Thus the twin functions of the tracheid have been divided between two specialized kinds of cell, resulting in both greater efficiency of water movement and greater strength. At times, the terms "hardwood" and "softwood" can be deceiving. Balsa wood, for example, has vessels and is technically a hardwood, but as any model-builder knows, it is much softer than pine, a true softwood.

It is the nature of a tree to be dying all the while it grows. Its woody xylem cells are made of a resilient carbohydrate material called cellulose, and of an even tougher substance called lignin. As a tree ages, the walls of the inner, older xylem cells are gradually infiltrated and thickened by deposits of the tree's waste products, including tannins, gums and resins. At length, the waste-impregnated cells can no longer conduct water up the tree and, in effect, die. As the central portion of the trunk fills with waste, it darkens and expands to form a core of heartwood. A young tree trunk consists mostly of living sapwood, while older trees have substantial heartwood cores. Chemical reactions among these wastes impart distinctive colors to different types of wood—the red-tinged brown of mahogany, for example, or the golden hue of oak.

Most wastes are produced in the outer sapwood near the cambium, where the process of growth is most intense, and are transported to the interior of the tree by cellular structures known as vascular rays. These lateral ribbons of cells can be seen in a cross section of a trunk, radiating from the center like the spokes of a bicycle wheel. The horizontally oriented rays not only carry waste, but also store food and carry it outward to the cambium layer when the cambial cells begin their work of dividing and reproducing.

The vascular cambium is present throughout the roots, producing xylem and phloem that thicken the roots and extending their tips at about the same pace as the branches grow overhead. If it were possible to measure the length of all the roots of a mature tree, the total would undoubtedly exceed several hundred miles, but only a small section of each root actively absorbs water and minerals. At the tip of each root, a tiny, hard cap functions somewhat like a drill bit as the root bores through the soil. Powered by cell growth immediately behind the cap, the tip pushes forward through soft soil with a screwlike movement; if a rock or some other impenetrable object is encountered, the tip turns aside and the root grows around the obstacle. Just behind the cap, along a section roughly the diameter of a piece of twine, thousands of one-celled root hairs grow at right angles to the root and absorb water and minerals. Typically, the root hairs remain active only for a few weeks; as the tip advances, new root hairs emerge just behind it, the older root hairs die, and their section of the root begins to expand. This expansion of the maturing root results in a wedging action, which increases the root system's grip on the soil.

As massive as the trunks and branches of great trees are aboveground, the root systems may be even larger. In fact, when a tree is young, the weight of the woody material in its root system is generally greater than the weight of the wood in the trunk and branches. But as the tree matures, the energy needed for growth lessens, as does the need for water and minerals from the soil. Thus, what scientists call the root-shoot ratio diminishes as the tree matures.

Even when the complexity of the tree's cellular organization has been grasped, and the elegance of the arboreal plumbing system understood, a

Barks of Distinction

Bark, a tree's armor against the elements, protects living tissues from extremes of heat and cold, insect attack, loss of moisture and even forest fires. For all its utilitarian nature, bark occurs in a dazzling variety of textures and colors, each the distinctive badge of a particular species of tree.

The outer bark, composed of fibers and dead, air-filled cells, cannot expand as the tree increases in girth; thus most kinds of bark crack, peel or flake as the tree grows. Trees such as the Chinese cherry (*below*) and birches shed their bark in papery layers, gradually exposing smooth new bark underneath. On other species, including the redwood (*right*) and the oaks, bark accumulates to great thicknesses, cracking in deep fissures as the trunk expands. Still other trees, including some pines, develop overlapping scales or plates of bark to accommodate their growth.

Factors that lend even more individuality to the barks of particular tree species include various pigments, etchings left by bark-boring insects, and lenticels—raised openings that allow air to reach the trees' living tissues.

CHINESE CHERRY sheds strips of old bark to expose the rich-hued fresh bark beneath.

REDWOOD bark up to a foot thick provides a formidable shield against insects and fires.

FLOSS SILK TREE is studded with spines—a defense against animals that eat its seeds.

RIVER BIRCH is clad in papery tatters of bark, formed as the outermost layers split and shed.

MANZANITA loses its outer bark in delicate curls that separate along the vertical bark fibers.

SITKA SPRUCE bares reddish new bark as older bark, lumpy with lenticels, flakes off.

PONDEROSA PINE, armored in interlocking plates, sheds old bark in tiny flakes.

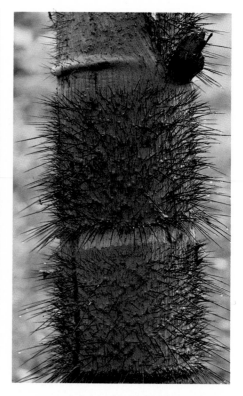

PEACH PALM bristles with needle-like spines that discourage animals from climbing the trunk.

BAOBAB has thick, seamed bark that contains fibers strong enough to be woven into rope.

CABBAGE PALMETTO bears the dagger-like bases of shed fronds along the length of its trunk.

CANARY ISLAND DATE PALM is scarred with the attachment points of fallen fronds.

SCRIBBLY GUM is clad in smooth bark patterned with the tracings of burrowing insect larvae.

MANNA GUM has long bark fibers that cause it to shed tough, persistent ribbons of bark.

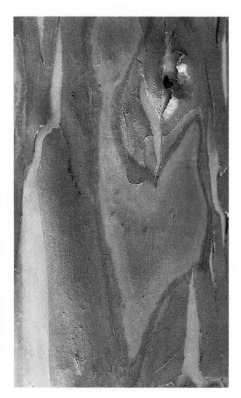

AUSTRALIAN GUM displays a changing palette of colors exposed in layers as old bark flakes off.

fundamental mystery remains: What force acts on the tree's vital supply of water to raise it to the leaves?

As early as the 17th Century, scientists knew that under certain circumstances the weight of the atmosphere would propel a liquid upward in apparent defiance of gravity. The process is frequently demonstrated with an open-ended glass tube and a water-filled pan: The experimenter fills the tube with water, seals one end with a finger and immerses the other end in the pan, then removes the finger. Some of the water in the tube always remains above the water level in the pan. To be sure, gravity is pulling the mass of the water in the tube downward, but it is also pulling earthward the less obvious but far greater mass of the atmosphere. The weight of the atmosphere exerts a larger total force on the broad surface of the water in the pan than it does on the small area in the tube; because of the differential, the water is pushed upward in the tube. Under ideal circumstances, as for instance when a suction pump removes much of the air from a closed pipe, atmospheric pressure can push a column of water to a maximum height of about 34 feet.

Conditions are far from ideal among the tiny vessels or tracheids of a tree trunk, and there is no apparent pump at work to help out, yet most mature trees are far more than 34 feet in height, and prodigious quantities of water make the long journey to the top. Each day during the growing season, an estimated 8,000 gallons of water evaporate from the leaves of one acre of beech and maple trees. The water is given off as vapor from tiny openings, or stomata, in the leaves. This process is called transpiration, and it has a dual significance: It is essential to the photosynthesis that provides the tree with its nourishment, and it is the key to the lifting of water all the way from the roots scores or hundreds of feet below.

Tiny bonds of attraction link water molecules to their neighbors. One manifestation of the cumulative effect of this bonding is surface tension, which allows certain insects to skate across a pond as if it were frozen. Molecular bonding links one water molecule to the next throughout the tree, forming a kind of chain. As leaves launch their billions of water molecules into the air, the molecular bonds draw other molecules upward in the sap to replace the departed vapor.

The pulling effect at each stoma is minuscule, but that of the tens of thousands of stomata on each of a large tree's complement of leaves can be enough to haul water upward at a rate of 200 feet per hour. Eventually, however, the force of gravity pulling downward on the mass of ascending water equals the total upward force of molecular bonding, and the water can rise no farther. (One reason that the leaves on the tops of the very tallest trees cease growing is the lack of sufficient water.) The mountain ash eucalyptus of Australia, which reaches 375 feet in height and is reputed to be the tallest tree variety in the world, probably represents the upper limit of the power of transpiration.

This remarkable system delivers to the leaves one of the raw materials required in their manufacture of food for the cells of the tree. However varied the shapes and sizes of leaves, from the three-foot-long giants on a West African tree called Anthocleista to the tiny leaflets of a locust tree, they all have the same basic equipment for their manufacturing task. The top of a leaf is covered by a membrane called the cuticle, a thin waxy layer that keeps the leaves from drying out. In dry climates, the leaf cuticle

Liquid Bounties from Living Wood

In many trees, ducts running through the sapwood and the phloem tissue that lies just beneath the outer bark carry resins and other viscous liquids that, unlike sap, contain no food or usable moisture for tree tissues. Scientists believe that the fluids, which harden on exposure to air, serve to seal wounds in the trunk and branches and prevent moisture loss. The pungent substances may also ward off decay and insect attack.

These specialized liquids have also proven to be useful to civilization. The milky latex that oozes from wounds in the bark of the rubber tree—native to South America and cultivated throughout the tropics—becomes raw rubber when it is chemically coagulated. In Europe, Asia and the American South, pine trees are tapped for resins that can be distilled to produce turpentine and rosin, a substance used in printing and soapmaking. Resins from other trees are harvested in smaller quantities around the world to provide ingredients for processed food, medicines and cosmetics. Earlier methods of tapping often killed the tree, but today's carefully gauged incisions allow a tree to remain productive for decades.

Unlike most such products, maple syrup originates not in a special resin but in ordinary sap. In early spring, starches stored in the wood of the maple tree are converted into sugars—fuel for new growth—and released into the water flowing upward through the sapwood. Spouts driven into the wood draw off this dilute sugar solution, and boiling concentrates it into a sweet essence.

A rope of latex dribbles from the bark of a rubber tree on a plantation in Malaysia. Every second day, workers trim a sliver of bark from the bottom of the bared strip to tap the tree, which exudes about five ounces of fluid before the latex congeals and stanches the flow.

Resin that will yield turpentine oozes down the exposed wood of a slash pine tree in Georgia. Sections of bark are periodically chipped away from the top of the bared patch to renew the flow of resin, while the lower part of the wound gradually heals over.

A metal spout embedded in a shallow hole near the base of a sugar maple in Ontario spills a drop of crystalline sap into a bucket. Thirty to 40 gallons of sap—the average annual yield of two trees—must be boiled down to produce one gallon of maple syrup.

may be relatively thick, an adaptation that retards the escape of precious water. In tropical rain forests, on the other hand, many trees not only possess thin cuticles, but they have also evolved drawn-out leaves with long, narrow tips, a kind of spout that permits water to run off more readily and allows the leaf to dry faster, thus compensating for abundant rainfall and high humidity.

Just below the cuticle lies a thin, one-cell-thick layer called the epidermis, which encloses the food-producing cells of the leaf's interior. The lower epidermis, on the underside of the leaf, is perforated by stomata—sometimes as many as 10,000 per square centimeter. Although the vast majority of trees have stomata only on the undersides of their leaves, some, including willows and poplars, have them on both sides. About the size of a pinprick, each stoma is flanked by two guard cells that act as valves. During the day, the guard cells shrink, widening the stoma and permitting gases from the atmosphere, most importantly carbon dioxide, to enter the leaves while water vapor and gases such as oxygen escape.

Sandwiched between the two epidermal layers, the tree's food factories bustle through their critical day shift. Just below the upper epidermis is a level of long, columnar cells called the palisade layer, a name taken from the cells' collective resemblance to the log walls, or palisades, of an old fort. Below the palisade layer is a spongy layer of loosely packed cells, threaded with veins, the distinctive branching lines—visible on all leaves—that are the outermost extensions of the tree's great plumbing system. Each vein is a tiny, two-tiered pipeline; the upper part contains xylem tissue, through which water arrives in the leaf, and the lower half is phloem, which carries manufactured sugars away. The veins also have a structural function: They are the supports that keep the leaf flat, presenting its full surface to the vital sunlight. Both the palisade layer and the spongy layer below it are riddled with air spaces between the cells; these are conduits for carbon dioxide coming into the plant and oxygen flowing out. Each cell of the interior layers contains chloroplasts, structures filled with minute deposits of a green pigment called chlorophyll. These give a leaf its characteristic color.

The light energy that penetrates to the chloroplasts through the thin, almost transparent epidermis excites the atoms of chlorophyll, and after a long and very complicated series of chemical reactions, is turned into chemical energy. The process acts on the water that is transported up from the soil by the xylem and on the carbon dioxide from the air diffused into the spaces between the leaf cells, transforming the two substances into complex organic molecules called carbohydrates; these nourish the cells of the tree while oxygen released as a by-product and water left over from the manufacturing process escape through the stomata. The carbohydrates are used first to fuel the growth of the leaf itself. When the leaf has reached its full growth, some of the carbohydrates it manufactures move into the phloem and are distributed to younger leaves and the rest of the tree's growing tissue.

The production of food from sunlight is without question the most important single chemical reaction on earth, for plant foodstuffs are basic to all forms of life. And the leaves of forest trees can be said to be the planet's most important producers of organic material, since more than four fifths of all plant tissue is contained in trees.

The Grand Design of a Tree

The trunk and limbs of a living tree are marvels of structural soundness, capable of sustaining a tree hundreds of feet tall through centuries of storms. But they also provide an intricate circulatory system that links the interdependent parts of the tree, supplying every one of its billions of living cells with water and minerals drawn from the roots and sugary food distributed from the leaves.

A cross section of a tree reveals two kinds of tissue encased by the outer bark, both threaded with tiny conducting cells but each specialized for different circulatory tasks. The narrow layer of soft, dark phloem just beneath the bark is the food-carrying tissue that circulates sugar-laden sap from the leaves. Beyond the phloem, separated from it by a layer of cells called the cambium, lies the xylem, the wood of the tree, patterned with annual growth rings.

Water and minerals percolate upward through the xylem, drawn from the roots through the trunk and limbs by a remarkable process that is powered by the evaporation of water from the leaves. As moisture flows into the leaf tissues to replace the liquid lost, the natural cohesiveness of water molecules transmits the motion all the way down the xylem tissue to the roots, drawing an entire column of water upward.

Phloem and xylem have other functions as well. Both contain starchy stores of food. And dead, desiccated cells from the phloem add to the protective layer of bark, while dead xylem adds to the heartwood at the core of the tree, a repository for resins, oils, tannins and other wastes from the tree's living tissues.

A cross section of a trunk shows the tissues that make up the tree's circulatory system, diagrammed here schematically. Water (blue) rises through the xylem as sap (yellow) descends through the phloem. The vascular rays that spoke the wood carry food and water laterally.

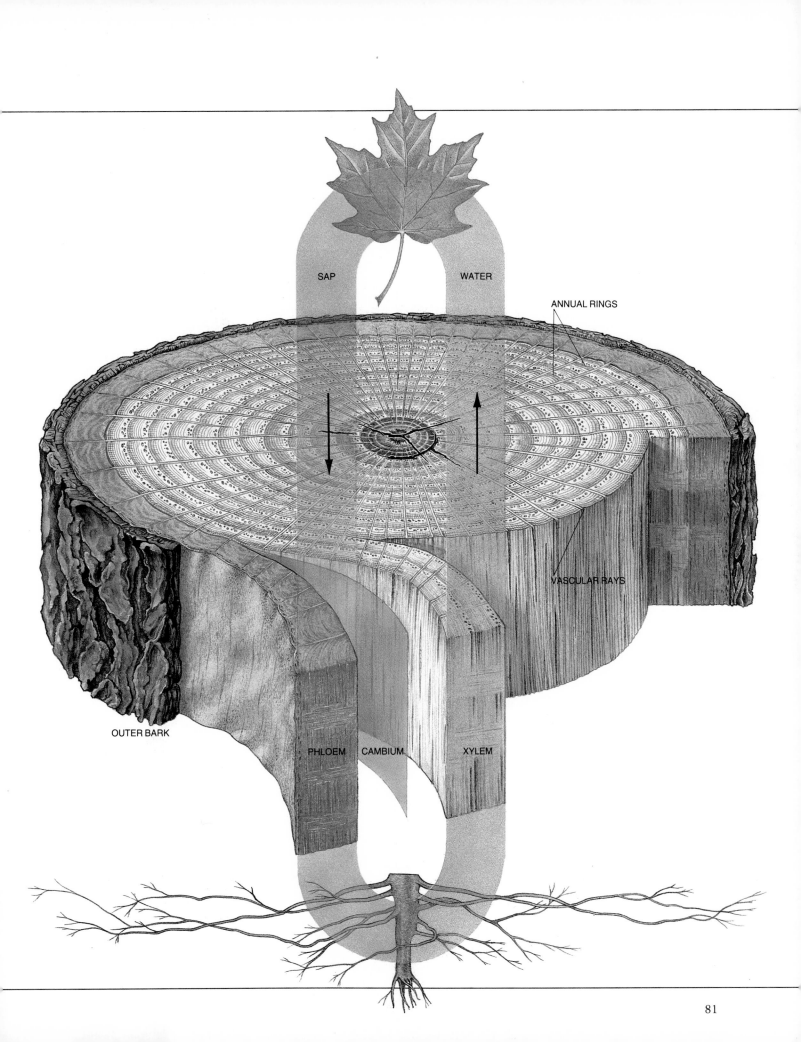

SAP

WATER

ANNUAL RINGS

VASCULAR RAYS

OUTER BARK

PHLOEM   CAMBIUM   XYLEM

Cells for Special Purposes

A microscopically thin layer of cells sandwiched between the phloem and the xylem is the source of all of the tons of woody growth that thicken a tree's trunk and limbs. Throughout the growing season, the cells of this layer, known as the cambium, divide to produce cellular offspring that gradually specialize, those on the outer side of the cambium adding to the phloem while those on the inner side contribute to the annual layer of new xylem that is visible in a cross section as a growth ring.

Another region of rapid growth lies underground, where the roots constantly extend new threads through the soil to keep the tree supplied with water and minerals. Behind the probing tip of each new rootlet sprout thousands of tiny root hairs that account for the vast absorptiveness of the root. Each hair grows to full length within a few hours, then dies back after a day or two as the root continues to extend. Some roots eventually thicken through the same process that produces wood aboveground.

The food that fuels these surging life processes is produced in the green cells of the leaves. There, billions of microscopic structures called chloroplasts, energized by sunlight, convert water and carbon dioxide into sugars and release oxygen as a by-product in a natural alchemy known as photosynthesis.

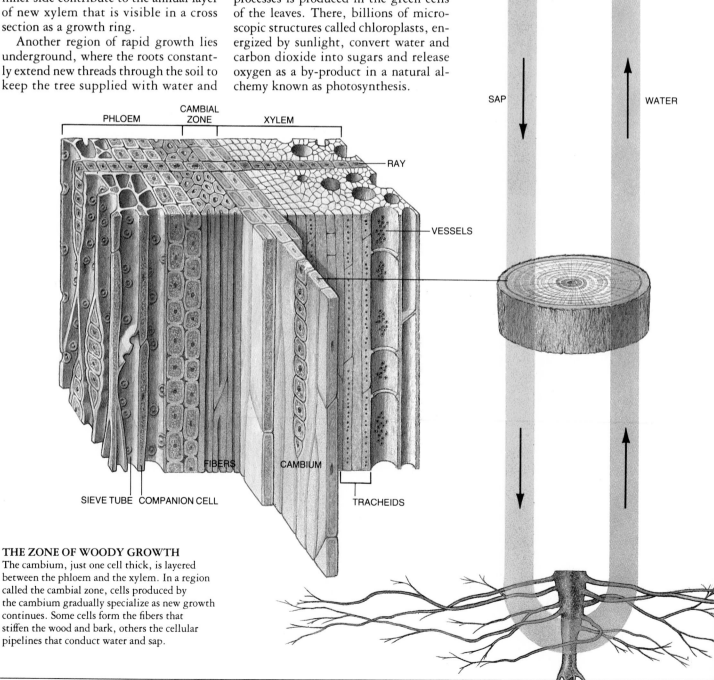

THE ZONE OF WOODY GROWTH
The cambium, just one cell thick, is layered between the phloem and the xylem. In a region called the cambial zone, cells produced by the cambium gradually specialize as new growth continues. Some cells form the fibers that stiffen the wood and bark, others the cellular pipelines that conduct water and sap.

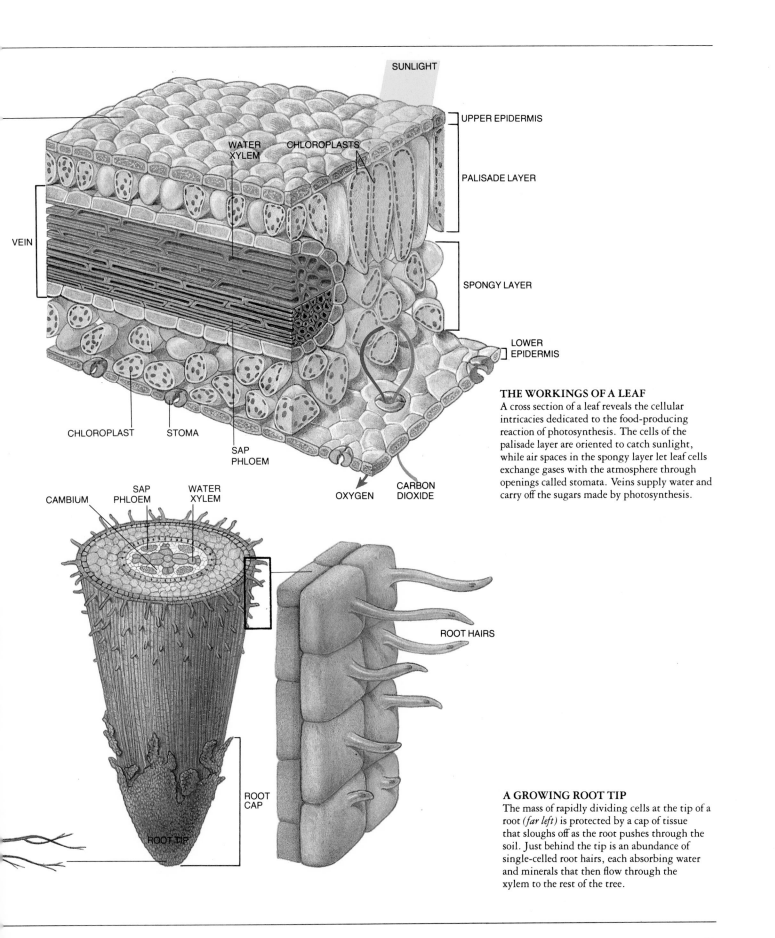

SUNLIGHT

UPPER EPIDERMIS

WATER XYLEM

CHLOROPLASTS

PALISADE LAYER

VEIN

SPONGY LAYER

LOWER EPIDERMIS

CHLOROPLAST

STOMA

SAP PHLOEM

OXYGEN

CARBON DIOXIDE

THE WORKINGS OF A LEAF
A cross section of a leaf reveals the cellular intricacies dedicated to the food-producing reaction of photosynthesis. The cells of the palisade layer are oriented to catch sunlight, while air spaces in the spongy layer let leaf cells exchange gases with the atmosphere through openings called stomata. Veins supply water and carry off the sugars made by photosynthesis.

CAMBIUM

SAP PHLOEM

WATER XYLEM

ROOT HAIRS

ROOT CAP

ROOT TIP

A GROWING ROOT TIP
The mass of rapidly dividing cells at the tip of a root (*far left*) is protected by a cap of tissue that sloughs off as the root pushes through the soil. Just behind the tip is an abundance of single-celled root hairs, each absorbing water and minerals that then flow through the xylem to the rest of the tree.

For all their importance, leaves are temporary fixtures. Even the so-called evergreens, including holly and magnolia, lose their leaves and replace them at a slow but constant rate so that the trees appear always to be more or less fully leaved. During Northern winters, when little or no moisture can be drawn up from the frozen ground to replace water lost through transpiration, the evergreens are nevertheless able to retain their leaves because the needles are coated with a thick, waxy film that inhibits water loss. Indeed, the individual needles of a red pine remain in place for about three years, while the balsam fir retains its needles for as long as seven years. Deciduous trees, of course, shed their leaves all at once every autumn. This abandonment of their food factories is a drastic strategy for survival dictated by environment and the merciless logic of evolutionary adaptation. The broad, thinly coated leaves of deciduous trees are far more wasteful of water than are evergreen needles, so leaf fall before winter is essential for survival. Without replacement for the water lost through transpiration in the leaves, the tree would quickly dry up and die. Instead, the leaves die, in an annual ritual that seems to paint many forests with the brilliant red, yellow and orange hues of autumn.

In fact, no tints are added to the leaves in this still-mysterious process; rather, the characteristic green of the chlorophyll is taken away. Chlorophyll pigment disintegrates with use, but during the growing season it is continuously replenished; in the fall, however, something interferes with its replacement, and the chlorophyll begins to disappear. As the green mantle vanishes, yellow and orange pigments called carotenoids—which have been present in the leaves all along and which are not broken down by the action of light—become visible. In addition, sugar in the leaves begins to turn into red and violet pigments called anthocyanins. As winter approaches, the supply of raw materials and water is finally choked off at the bases of the leaf stems, and the leaves fall off. The barren tree then enters a dormant state and virtually hibernates through the winter.

When warmer temperatures and longer days return, a complex series of events commences in the tissues that are known collectively as meristem. Found in all parts of a tree, meristematic cells are those that have the capacity to divide and thereby reproduce themselves. The vascular cambium, which adds xylem and phloem to the roots, trunk and major limbs, is one kind of meristem; another form extends the root tips into the soil; a third is present in the tips of stems and branches. Drawing on the tree's stored supplies of food, the meristem begins its reproductive work first in the stem tips, where cells divide and begin to elongate. Some of these new cells become xylem and phloem, extending the stem's length; others differentiate into the constituent cells of leaves.

The intense chemical activity involved in growth produces a number of by-products, the most important of which are vitamins and hormones. Vitamins, present in most forms of life, are organic substances that have an indirect role in the processes that convert food to energy or cell formation. Animals produce very few vitamins in their cells, humans only one—vitamin D, formed in the skin by the action of sunlight. Trees and other plants, however, manufacture the entire range of vitamin substances.

The essential role of vitamins in regulating metabolism is relatively well understood, but considerable mystery still surrounds the workings of hormones. Like vitamins, hormones are organic compounds that influence life

A maple leaf begins to redden as the cooler weather of autumn slows the sap movement that carries newly synthesized sugars from the leaves. The sugars accumulate in the leaves and, when exposed to sunlight, change to bright pigments. A portion of this leaf that has been in the shade retains its summer color.

processes in subtle but profound ways. Their chemical nature and their effects on the workings of trees have been the subject of much research since they were discovered around the turn of the century. Several kinds of plant hormones have been identified; some mediate the processes that cause flowers and fruits to form, others dictate when leaves and fruits fall off the tree. But the most intriguing to scientists are the ones that regulate growth. Some tree hormones promote growth, others inhibit it; a few function either way, depending upon the season. Changes in the balance of these hormones dictate the onset of dormancy in the fall and the burst of growth in the spring.

One of the most fascinating hormone types, the auxins, are primarily responsible for the tendency of trees to bend toward light, a trait known as heliotropism. Synthesized in the meristem tissues in the tips of young leaves or newly opening buds, auxins migrate to any part of a growing stem that is shaded, and cause the cells there to elongate faster; auxins are inactivated by light, so the well-lighted part of the stem grows more slowly, if at all. The result of the differing influences is that the stem curves toward the light as it grows.

The meristem, which accounts for a tree's growth and produces its hormones, has one other all-important function. Reacting to a variety of factors such as temperature, the amount of sunlight and the availability of water, and to its own inherent patterns of growth, the meristem at certain times turns to the task of preparing for reproduction—the manufacture of male and female sex organs. The process is essentially the same for the flowering trees, or angiosperms, and the gymnosperm, or naked seed, varieties such as the pines.

Most of the woody cones that litter the ground under a pine tree are female cones, which often grow on the tips of branches. For their first year or so, the female cones' scales remain soft and open, exposing the ovules. Each ovule is wrapped in an integument, or protective layer; hidden in each ovule is an egg cell. In the spring, the male cones, which are usually smaller and are produced lower down on the branches, release their pollen and die. Each pollen grain is a little packet of sperm that also contains other, specialized cells. Borne by the wind, some of the pollen grains eventually make contact with the ovule, whereupon the specialized cells begin to form a pollen tube that extends toward the egg. When the tube has formed, the sperm moves through it to fertilize the egg. In pines, a full year may elapse between pollination and fertilization.

The basic difference in the reproductive process of flowering trees is that the eggs of angiosperms are enclosed in a protective ovary, from which in most flowers a tubular growth called the style extends. On the end of the style is an organ called the stigma, which receives the pollen grain from a male flower or from male organs in the same flower. When the pollen germinates, the pollen tube grows down the length of the style until it reaches the egg. Fertilization usually takes place within a few days and the ovary begins to mature into a ripened fruit. Most fruits, such as apples, peaches and berries, are fleshy and carry their seeds in special compartments, or in a stone or pit surrounded by a fleshy layer and a skin. Birds and animals attracted by the fruit often help to disperse the seeds. But other fruits, among them such nuts as acorns and chestnuts, are dry, and locust trees have capsule-like fruit that opens when the seeds are ripe to allow the seeds to fall to the ground.

The life span of trees varies greatly among species. The eastern white pine, for example, can live for as long as 500 years, while few loblolly pines survive for half that long. Beech trees sometimes live for 400 years, but the gray birch has a life expectancy of only 50 years. The oldest trees on earth are bristlecone pines, which eke out life spans of some 4,000 years in the dry American Southwest.

The struggle to adapt to many different environments has led to some remarkable variations on the basic themes of tree architecture. Long periods of isolation, for example on oceanic islands, have sometimes given rise to arboreal plants that are barely recognizable as trees. Herbaceous relatives of such low-growing plants as lettuce, beets, cucumbers and daisies have evolved into treelike forms and even into what could be called forests. This evolutionary process is called adaptive radiation; a plant species finding itself in a place where there is relatively little competition tends, over time, to evolve new forms that take advantage of the situation.

The tarweeds of California and Hawaii illustrate the phenomenon. When this shrubby plant arrived on the Hawaiian Islands from the mainland (its sticky seeds no doubt borne there by migratory birds), it exploded opportunistically into a host of varieties. One of them, the silver sword—a small, bristling ball of ivory-colored leaves—thrives on the bare lava of volcanic cinder cones, where dryness and extreme heat and cold are the norm. Meanwhile, a relative has evolved into a broad-leaved tree that grows more than

86

Exploring a Tree's Miniature Cosmos

After examining the structure of wood with an early microscope, a 17th Century scientist declared that the intricate material was "a piece of Nature's Handicraft, which far surpasses the most elaborate Woof or Needle Work in the World." Modern microscopes can reveal even finer detail in wood and other tree tissues, thus opening a hidden domain of otherworldly beauty.

The photographs on this and the following pages were taken with scanning electron microscopes, devices that produce an image by playing a beam of electrons across the surface of a specimen. The pattern of electrons reflected from surface irregularities is amplified, then projected on a television screen or recorded on film at magnifications of 20,000 times and more. To increase the reflectivity of substances such as wood and leaf tissue, samples are coated with a whisper-thin layer of metal—usually an alloy of gold and the rare element palladium.

This technique produces eerie but realistic glimpses of the minute topography of tree tissues. Appearing three-dimensional because of the crisp definition and varying textures, the images depict the tiniest details of the intricate workings of a tree: the vessels that pipe water and minerals through the wood, the mouthlike stomata through which leaf tissues exchange gases with the atmosphere and the lilliputian aerodynamics of windborne pollen grains.

Magnified about 125 times, a cross section of red oak wood encompasses portions of two annual growth rings. The dense wood in the foreground, pricked with tiny vessels, was produced in late summer; the new growth of the following spring is honeycombed with broad vessels that channeled large quantities of water to developing leaves.

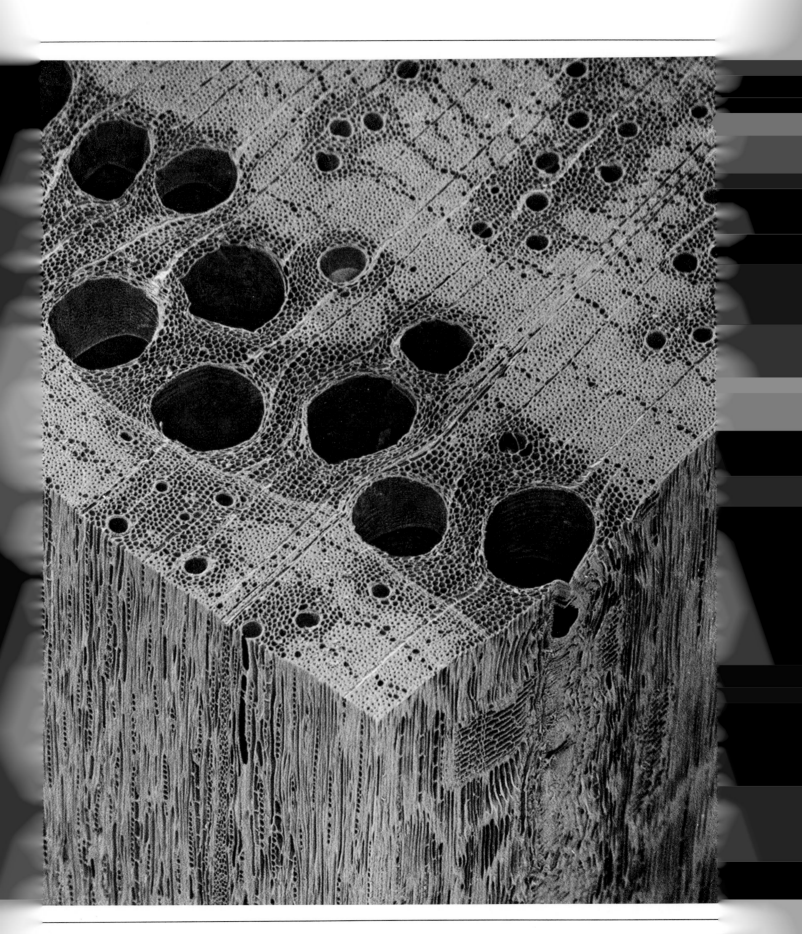

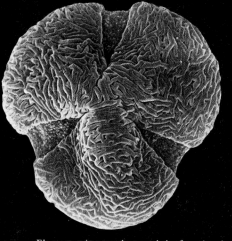

Leaf hairs bristle among the stomata on the veined underside of an elm leaf that has been enlarged 125 times. The hairs probably serve to slow the movement of air across the leaf, thus reducing the rate of evaporative water loss.

Enlarged about 2,800 times in this cross section, a stoma opens downward into a pine needle beneath a pursed lip of protective tissue. The cells on either side of the stoma vary the size of the opening by swelling or shrinking, thus regulating the flow of gases between internal tissues and the open air.

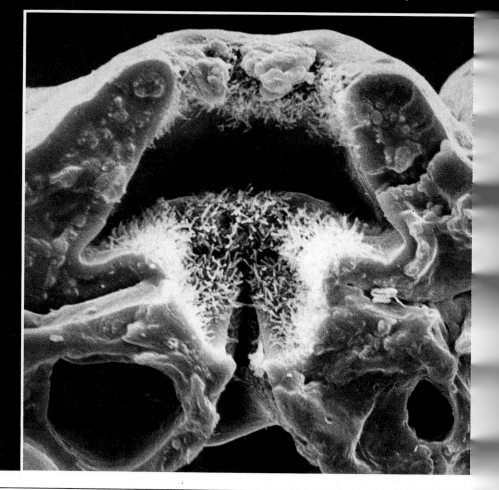

Electron micrographs reveal the functional intricacies of pollen grains from a white pine, enlarged 2,400 times *(top)*, and a box elder, enlarged 1,820 times *(above)*. Twin air sacs on the pine pollen help it catch the wind; the box elder pollen is seamed with furrows along which it splits as it fertilizes an egg.

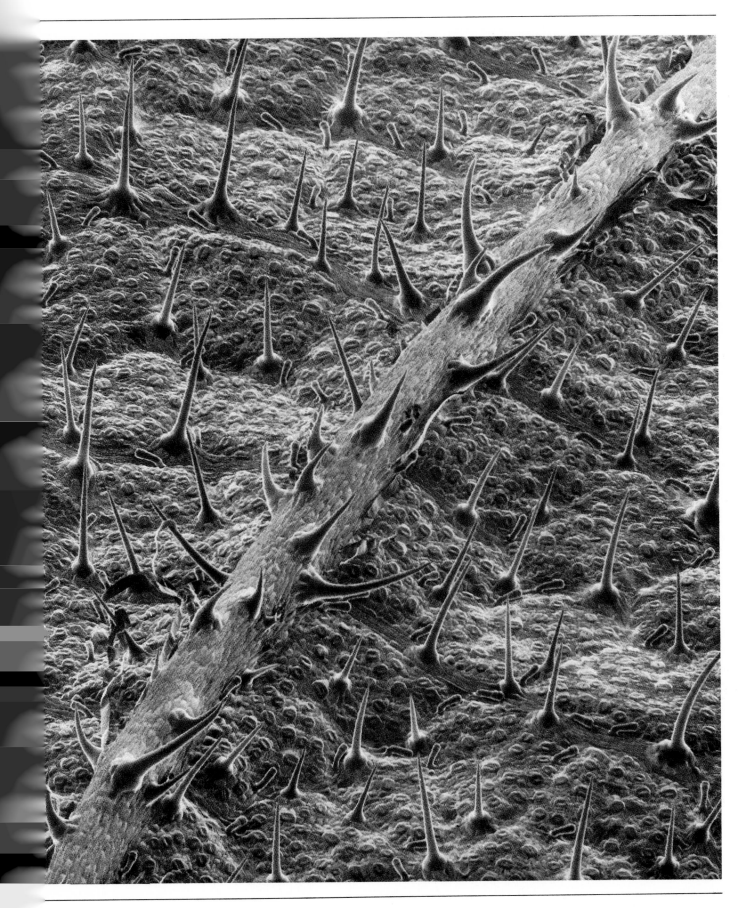

20 feet tall in the islands' rain forests, where rainfall sometimes exceeds 500 inches per year.

The different forms that can be assumed by a tree's basic components—roots, trunk and leaves—are almost countless. The baobab tree of the African savanna, for example, is not much more than 50 feet tall, but its trunk is swollen to nearly the girth of a California redwood's. The tall, slim trunks of many tropical trees, growing in thin soil with small underground root systems, would have an extremely precarious life if it were not for the evolutionary modification of the roots into high, aboveground buttresses. A number of tree types have aerial roots; screw pines and mangroves have roots that grow from stems on the trunk and reach the soil obliquely, like the poles of a tepee frame. The roots of some fig trees, including the great banyan trees that are native to India, hang down from long lateral branches. When these tendrils reach the ground, they may grow larger than the trunks of many other trees. So extensive are the lateral branches and descending roots of the banyan tree that it has been called a one-tree forest. One banyan in India grew to cover three acres.

Any tree, especially a sprawling banyan tree or a tall, gracefully spreading oak, creates and sustains its own special microclimate. The moisture from transpiration cools the air nearby, while deep shade prevents life-giving sunlight from nourishing most forms of undergrowth. Trees are by their nature gregarious, and the more trees there are, the more pronounced their influence on the environment. Conditions fluctuate less widely in forests than in adjacent open areas. Forests tend to be darker and distinctly cooler than nearby meadows or fields. A dense and widespread tree cover also reduces wind drastically: The wind speed in a pine forest with trees about 45 feet high is only one quarter the wind speed above the canopy, and the taller the forest, the greater the reduction. Thus forests are unique habitats that favor certain creatures and, of course, discourage others.

Indeed, in the planetary household—and the word "ecology" derives from the Greek word for "household"—forests are a major part of the global ventilation system that maintains conditions favorable to life. Along with its oceans, the world's forests play a major role in absorbing carbon dioxide in the atmosphere, the result of the exhalations of animal life and more recently of the burning of fossil fuels. After consuming the carbon dioxide they need for growth, forests expel enormous quantities of oxygen into the atmosphere, helping to maintain the oxygen level conducive to life. At a time when more and more fossil fuel is being burned, and ever-larger areas are being deforested, many scientists have become concerned about the possibility of a build-up of excess carbon dioxide in the atmosphere. Carbon dioxide tends to trap solar heat that would otherwise radiate back out to space, in what is referred to as the greenhouse effect, and scientists worry that if too much carbon dioxide accumulates, the global climate will become warmer. An increase of only a few degrees in average world temperatures could have a profound effect on the earth's ecosystems.

In their distribution and character, forests reflect the sensitivity of their constituent trees to environmental conditions. Large portions of the earth have no forests. They are too dry, too wet, too exposed, too cold, or too high. Where forests do appear, they vary widely, depending on the local climate and topography.

Like all living things, a forest depends on solar radiation. Yet only a

Short-stalked flowers and fruit spring directly from the trunk and main limbs of a cocoa tree in a tropical jungle. Most trees form their flowers on small leafy branches, but this adaptation to conditions in the jungle's dark understory makes the flowers more visible and may attract more insect pollinators.

The white root of a germinating horse chestnut reaches for the water and mineral supply in the soil below. The husk that enclosed the seed was split off by the expansion of the root and the two seed leaves inside the chestnut.

fraction of the sunlight streaming down on the forest canopy, the leafy ceiling that is usually the densest part of the vegetation, is used in photosynthesis. The leaves reflect more than half of the sun's energy back into the atmosphere and absorb almost half of the remainder as heat, which drives the process of water evaporation and is therefore also returned to the atmosphere. Only about 2 per cent of the radiant solar energy that strikes a forest is used in plant production—that is, the building of roots, stems and leaves. About half of this modest portion of energy is soon released into the air as heat, which is generated by the chemical processes of growth. And the minute portion of solar energy that is transformed by photosynthesis into tissue is eventually returned to the earth, either when the tree dies and decomposes, or when the leaves fall.

The forests' cyclical processing of solar energy sustains an even more complex biological cycle. Through its fallen leaves, the forest helps to replenish its own nitrogen; bacteria and fungi in the soil consume the litter and in the process turn nitrogen into nitrates, which can be used by the trees. The microorganisms themselves provide food for invertebrate animals

Sitka spruce trees straddle the decaying log on which they sprouted, in the rain forest of Washington's Olympic Peninsula. Such "nurse logs," as they are called, in many places offer the only spots dry enough for tree seeds to germinate; here the forest soil is kept sodden by an annual rainfall of 145 inches.

such as insects and worms, which in turn provide food for other creatures. And the interplay of solar energy and living forms extends still further, to the herbivores that live on the forest's vegetation and the predators that feed upon the plant eaters.

Human fascination with the forest ecosystem is endless and elemental. Descended from creatures that dwelled in trees millions of years ago, humans have for hundreds of thousands of years made abundant use of wood in their weapons, tools and shelters. Perhaps this long relationship explains the response our species has to trees and wood. The architect Frank Lloyd Wright called wood "the most humanly intimate of all materials. Man loves his association with it, likes to feel it under his hand. Wood is universally beautiful to Man." This emotional affinity is vividly summed up by an entry in the diary of a plainswoman who lived in Kansas in the late 1800s. "When Mr. Hilton, a pioneer, told his wife that he was going to Little River for wood, she asked to go with him," the diarist noted. "She hadn't seen a tree for two years, and when they arrived at Little River, she put her arms around a tree and hugged it until she was hysterical." Ω

ARBOREAL SCULPTURES

The shapes of most trees are variations on two basic themes: the conical outline typical of evergreens and the slender trunk and spreading crown of broad-leaved trees. But trees that grow under unusual circumstances sometimes form unexpected, strangely beautiful living sculptures.

Trees rooted near one another may twist together or even fuse, if contact between the trunks wears away bark and allows layers of living cells to merge. In arctic and alpine regions, the harsh environment can reduce a tree to a stunted caricature of its usual form, while a tree flourishing under ideal conditions may gain a bizarre aspect as its limbs spread and twist in untrammeled vigor.

Other peculiarities characterize entire groups of trees. The grass trees of Australia owe their improbable appearance to the fact that they are not conventional trees at all but relatives of the lily, while the baobab trees of Africa and counterparts in Australia have adapted to arid habitats by developing trunks that are grotesquely swollen with stored water.

Tormented by mountaintop weather in Yosemite National Park, California, the twisted limbs of a Jeffrey pine grow with the prevailing wind.

The trunks of a pair of tropical trees of the baobab family entwine in a ponderous *pas de deux* on the island of Madagascar.

An enormous cypress near Oaxaca, Mexico, incorporates three separate trees that grew together and fused centuries ago. The trunk's 138-foot girth is the largest of any known tree.

A baobab looms over the grasslands of Kenya. The base of this species of tree, which can attain a circumference of 90 feet, contains spongy wood that is capable of storing up to 25,000 gallons of water.

Spirelike flower stalks crown the shaggy foliage of a grass tree in the Australian scrub forest. The trunk and branches consist not of wood but of tightly packed leaf bases bonded together by a tough, resinous secretion.

The bottle tree of Australia, like the
similarly rotund baobab, depends on stores of
water in the spongy wood of the bulbous
trunk to sustain the tree through long droughts.

The largest live oak in the United States, on
Johns Island, South Carolina, spreads angular
limbs across a span of 160 feet. The oak
may have lived for as long as 1,500 years—five
times the normal life span of live oaks.

Aerial roots cascade from the limbs of a curtain fig tree in an Australian rain forest. These myriad roots will thicken and merge into a smaller number of massive supports.

A Gallery of Roots

Roots contain the same wood-producing tissues as trunks and limbs and are as distinctive and elaborate as the rest of tree architecture. But only in the case of a few species, or peculiar circumstances, can they be seen.

Some of the most dramatic of visible roots are the so-called aerial roots that descend from outlying branches of various species of fig trees. Growing earthward as mere threads at first, these roots eventually develop into stout auxiliary trunks that enable a single tree to extend its canopy of leaves to cover an enormous area.

When a conventional tree takes hold in thin, rocky soil, its main roots may be forced aboveground as they thicken, or erosion may strip away topsoil to expose the gnarled intricacies of the tree's root system.

Swollen by centuries of growth, the knotted roots of a limber pine bulk above the surface of the shallow soil on a mountainside in California.

Aerial roots shore up the branches of a banyan tree, a species of fig whose buttressed crown of foliage can measure as much as 600 feet across.

Chapter 4

THE PULSE OF TEMPERATE WOODLANDS

From a spot near the western shore of Canada's Hudson Bay, not far from the town of Churchill, Manitoba, the view to the north is virtually unobstructed to the distant horizon. And beyond the range of sight, all the way to the North Pole and then on for a thousand miles, only a few stunted and twisted arctic willows punctuate the bleak landscape. The town of Churchill, located at lat. 65° N., lies on the tree line—a globe-girdling boundary, nudged into serpentine undulations here and there by local climatic and geologic conditions, that marks the northernmost edge of the world's great temperate forests. To the north lie tundra and ice, to the south, woodlands that cover some four billion acres—about one eighth of the land on earth.

Made up almost exclusively of coniferous trees in the higher latitudes and of deciduous trees in warmer regions, these sprawling temperate forests flourish primarily in the Northern Hemisphere, where vast land masses are subject to dramatic seasonal changes. South of the Equator, only the tips of Africa and South America dip below the subtropics. (Australia, governed by its own peculiar combination of subtropical and temperate environments, hosts extensive forests of eucalyptus trees, which cannot tolerate subfreezing temperatures.)

Despite the extent of the Northern forests, they are only remnants of the woodlands that once blanketed the planet. As recently as 8,000 years ago, oak, pine and laurel trees covered most of the lands around the Mediterranean Sea, including Spain, southern France and Greece; today, this once-lush expanse is in large part cloaked by a dense, shrubby growth known as maqui. Deciduous forests stretched over much of Western and Central Europe, and into Russia as far as the Ural Mountains; now much of this land has been turned to agricultural and industrial use. The story is similar in China. Overall, the evidence indicates that 80 centuries ago, the world's temperate forests were at least three times their present size.

Most of this reduction has occurred in relatively recent times, largely because of fire and human activities. But in the distant past, a succession of ice ages undoubtedly caused even greater destruction to Northern temperate forests. As mile-thick ice sheets advanced southward in Europe and North America, many Northern forests were virtually erased. The damage from the latest ice age is still apparent in Europe. Invading from the North some 100,000 years ago, the ice sheets and glaciers trapped many large forests against the Alps and the Pyrenees, which blocked the migration of seeds into more hospitable lands to the south. Falling on the barren upslope soils, or in areas already thickly settled by sturdier vegetation, the seeds of many

Stands of conifers and autumn-gilded aspens interlace on a Colorado mountainside that has been dusted by an early snowfall. The conjunction of seasonal change and diverse vegetation produces endless variations in temperate forests.

species failed to germinate. Consequently, even though most of the great forests regenerated when the ice retreated, only about a thousand species of trees are found in modern Europe. The tree population of North America fared far better in the face of the advancing ice sheets because the north-south orientation of the continent's mountain ranges allowed seeds to find fertile ground in warmer regions. Today, some 3,000 tree species thrive in North American forests. And in China, which was not extensively glaciated, almost all types of the world's temperate trees can be found.

The withdrawal of the ice sheets and the moderating of the global climate permitted the tree line to migrate northward to its present location near the Arctic Circle. The first sign of forestation to the south of the tree line is usually the widely spaced trees of the zone called the taiga, a broad belt of coniferous forest that sprawls across all of the Northern continents.

Sturdy, prolific and well adapted to a variety of environmental conditions, conifers are one of the most abundant types of tree on earth. On North America's West Coast, soaring redwoods grow as far south as Monterey, California, and the Eastern conifers blanket the Maritime Provinces and cover large tracts in 16 states; from England and Scandinavia, the swath of coniferous forests extends almost 12,000 miles across Europe and the Soviet Union to the shores of the Bering Sea.

Conifers reign unchallenged in the coldest and most forbidding regions, north of about lat. 55° N. The northernmost conifers of all appear in eastern Siberia near lat. 70° N. These hardy trees are larches, one of the few species able to stand picket along the edge of the frigid, empty tundra. The larches survive in the coldest areas because, unlike most evergreens, they shed all their needles each year just before winter, thus reducing moisture loss and minimizing the damage done by high wind and heavy snow. Larches at the

A map depicts the natural domains of the major types of forest found in the world today. Forests have adapted to virtually every latitude outside the polar regions of ice and tundra.

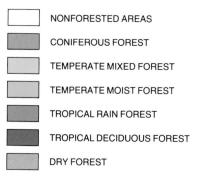

NONFORESTED AREAS

CONIFEROUS FOREST

TEMPERATE MIXED FOREST

TEMPERATE MOIST FOREST

TROPICAL RAIN FOREST

TROPICAL DECIDUOUS FOREST

DRY FOREST

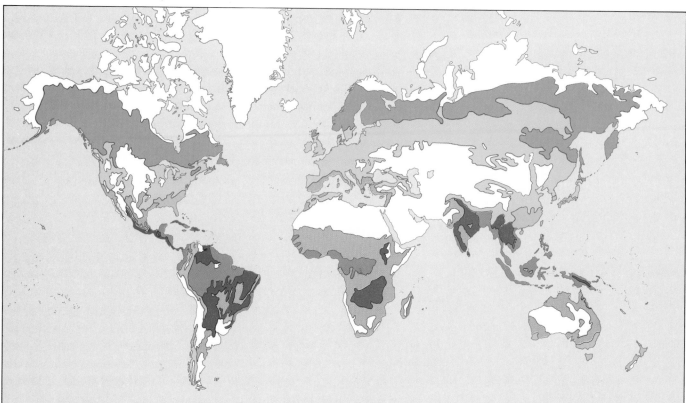

tree line in the taiga grow much more slowly than other conifers; some Siberian trees have 60 growth rings per inch of trunk diameter, a rate of growth about one tenth that of a conifer in the Southern United States.

Although growth may be extraordinarily slow near the tree line, the extensive forests a little farther to the south attest to the overall success of the hardy conifers in a harsh and frigid realm. In such places, trees must be able to withstand long periods of cold and drought, endure the damaging effects of wind and snow, and do their growing in a season that is only three or four months long. And as if this were not challenge enough, these forests must depend on some of the world's poorest soils—the rocky shavings left behind by the retreating glaciers of the Ice Age.

In a sense, the soil is further impoverished by the trees themselves. Evergreen needles are acidic. When they fall, accumulate on the forest floor and slowly decompose, they form a layer of black, acid humus just below the surface. The acid, seeping downward with rain water, leaches valuable mineral nutrients out of the root zone in the soil below the humus. Too poor to harbor earthworms and other soil-mixing creatures, the sandy soil soon becomes so hard that the trees' roots have difficulty pushing through it in search of water and nutrients.

Such conditions, combined with the effects of long winters and short growing seasons, would make tree growth virtually impossible were it not for the fact that conifers have useful companions in the soil. Certain kinds of fungi living among the trees' root hairs rapidly extract minerals from the decomposing litter and transfer the nutrients to the roots, which in turn provide the fungi with carbohydrates. This symbiotic relationship has been shown to increase a young pine tree's growth rate by some 20 per cent.

Aboveground, the conifers display other traits that adapt them to the harsh northern climate. Their supple branches flex to allow heavy loads of snow to slide off harmlessly, and a waxy coating on their needles reduces moisture loss in winter. With their narrow leaves, which expose far less surface area than broad leaves, conifers are well adapted to survive desiccating winter winds, and because evergreens (with the exception of larches) retain their leaves year round, these conifers can burst into photosynthetic action as soon as the length of the day and temperature become favorable. Typically, pines become active when the temperature reaches 52° F.

The most familiar temperate-zone evergreens—pines, firs, hemlocks, cypresses, spruces, cedars, redwoods and junipers—reigned long before the first deciduous trees ventured a leaf, and they still hold the records for size and longevity. No deciduous tree grows taller than 200 feet, but some conifers, especially California's redwood giants, exceed 250 feet: The tallest ever found was a coast redwood measuring 367 feet—62 feet taller than the Statue of Liberty. Many conifers, including the Sierra redwoods and the cedars of Lebanon, live for a thousand years or more, and the Rocky Mountains' bristlecone pines are the oldest trees in the world; some were seedlings when the Egyptian pharaohs started the great pyramids.

Although many types of evergreens are prized for their lumber, the pines are probably the most abundant—and thus the most important in economic terms. The Scots pine was the only pine to survive Northern Europe's glaciation and is today the most widely distributed pine in the world. It flourishes in a great belt stretching from Scotland eastward to the Pacific Ocean, and from Finland south to Spain and Turkey. The North

American counterparts of the Scots pine are white pine and Southern pines.

At about lat. 55° N. are found the northernmost deciduous woodlands. The first significant groups of broad-leaved trees, mostly willows, poplars and birches, begin to dapple the coniferous woodlands of the Northern Hemisphere in lower Scandinavia and near the northern border of the Great Lakes in North America. Farther south, the forests are dominated by such trees as oak, hickory, beech and maple; in all, about 2,500 species of deciduous trees can be found in an area that extends as far south as Florida and Mexico in North America and the city of Canton in China. Germany's legendary Black Forest, Sherwood Forest in England, and the Forest of Fontainebleau near Paris are all primarily broad-leaved woodlands.

There is a melancholy, almost unnatural stillness to a deciduous forest in winter. The tree trunks rise black and gaunt from the snow like soiled bones, while here and there tangles of dry vines and skeletal shrubs draw the eye upward toward a few desiccated leaves, dead but not fallen.

But as lifeless and forbidding as it may seem, the winter landscape is in fact a vital starting point for the dynamic workings of the forest's perennial cycle. Indeed, the ceaseless seasonal stirrings of the great midlatitude forests of Asia, Europe and North America seem almost frenetic compared with the stately fastness of evergreen woodlands.

From towering oaks to the Arctic's dwarf willow, which is only a few inches tall at maturity, all deciduous trees discard their food-producing leaves in the fall. (Yet even before they cast off one year's leaves, they have prepared within tiny buds the infant leaves that will once more bedeck the trees in spring.) The remarkable and often spectacular leaf fall represents an adaptive tradeoff: The trees shed their leaves to avoid moisture loss during a season when little or no water can be siphoned from frozen ground. The

Stunted by a brief growing season and desiccating winds, Engelmann's spruces struggle to survive at an altitude of 12,000 feet in the Colorado Rockies. Just above them, the timberline, which is sharply demarcated on the peaks in the background, indicates where conditions become too harsh for seedlings to develop.

Twenty-foot-high conifers slump beneath their heavy burdens of snow in California's Lassen Volcanic National Park. Snow seldom damages the resilient boughs of evergreens; in fact, it helps to shield them from drying sunshine and insulates them from the cold.

largeness of deciduous leaves provides increased food-making capability, which in part compensates for the growth time lost while the tree is leafless.

Still, winter does bring death to the deciduous forest. Few insects survive the cold. Annual plants die, of course, and even some young tree shoots and saplings succumb to freezing winds. In very cold weather, the water in small limbs may freeze, damaging cell membranes: If many cells perish, the limb may die. Most trees, however, endure the cold months in a state akin to hibernation, much as some forest animals do. Having turned off their food production by shedding their leaves, the trees accumulate sugars in root and bark cells. Belowground, metabolic activity in the roots decreases, and in the frozen soil countless insect larvae and the bulbs and underground stems of perennial plants await the spring.

With the coming of longer, warmer days, the forest floor begins to stir. Tiny herbs such as spring beauties and trout lilies, along with many small trees, race through their flowering stage before the taller trees unfurl new leaves and shut off the sunlight. Birds return from warmer climes to gorge themselves and feed their young on juicy earthworms and slugs. In the late spring, the tallest trees finally don their foliage, and the forest comes alive in the splendid annual birthing, a time of palpable vigor, of extravagant

fertility. The transformation is elegant: The hillsides and gullies recently etched with bleak shadows are now benign, soft, and alive with noise.

In the late spring and early summer, conditions for growth are at their best. The air and soil are warmest, and the pulse of the forest, from the tops of the trees to the subsoil, is quickest. In high summer, insects feast upon the lush foliage and fill the warm nights with a shrill cacophony. As bugs nibble away at the food-producing leaves, trees compete fiercely for the nourishing sunlight: The lower trees must often settle for a slow-growth season as the larger trees cast them into shadow. If there is ample rainfall, plant growth is riotous and tree rings will be thick and hearty. However, if a drought develops, the forest's metabolism slows, and the annual growth rings of trees will be narrow. Predictably, drought also increases the danger that the orderly procession of seasonal changes will be disrupted by wildfire.

The brisk pace of forest life begins to ease before the warmest days are past. As days become shorter and nights cooler, the decline toward winter dormancy begins. The magnificent fall display of colors marks the end of food production in the leaves, and as the green chlorophyll breaks down, brilliant red, yellow and purple hues present in residual foodstuffs create a vivid palette before the leaves drop off to reveal the sobering winterscape.

As a result of human intervention, the seasonal pageant of the deciduous woodlands does not take place in some of the warmer regions of the United States. Instead of graceful beeches, maples and oaks, great pine forests cover the states that made up the old Confederacy. The Civil War, in fact, played a major role in changing the make-up of Southern forests; much of the South had been cleared for agriculture, especially the lucrative cotton crop, which soon exhausted the soil. With the victory of the Union Army and the end of slavery, many of the great plantations fell into disuse. Soil that would not support cotton turned out to be excellent for pine trees, which require fewer soil nutrients. By the 1890s, the former plantations had become great forests of loblolly, slash, longleaf and shortleaf pine.

Deliberate planting of these trees was a major goal of work programs sponsored by the government in the 1930s, and more planting was done after World War II. In time, these Southern pine forests became one of the great wood baskets of the world. The mild climate and the generally level topography promote rapid growth, and foresters have learned how to nurture the trees and accelerate it even more. In the 19th Century, for example, a sapling might have taken 60 years to reach maturity; 100 years later, a tree-farm sapling was expected to reach its full size within about 40 years.

Near Florida's Lake Okeechobee, the Southern pines in turn give way to subtropical trees such as pond cypress and palmetto. The trees here are not subject to the frigid and fickle climate of the temperate zones, but many of them, responding to seasonal droughts, still shed their leaves late in the fall. Curiously, no pine trees are native to the Southern Hemisphere, but trees similar in appearance to pines are widespread in South America, Africa and Australia. Although not of the same family as true pines, the Australian hoop pine and the Chile pine—both coniferous evergreens—were mistakenly called pines when they were discovered. The Chile pine was exported to Europe and became popular in Victorian England, where it was nicknamed the monkey puzzle tree because, it was said, even a monkey would be confused climbing on the tree's contorted and interwoven branches.

In southern Brazil, the candelabra tree flourishes. A conifer with long,

A barren forest floor in Finland testifies to the infertile soil of coniferous forests. As they decay, fallen needles release acids, leaching out minerals that are vital to undergrowth.

tuft-tipped branches reminiscent of its namesake ornament, it grows to an average height of 100 feet and is a valuable source of lumber. The Patagonian cypress is the monarch of the southern Andes mountains. Its wood is similar to that of the California redwood, and it lives almost as long. In South Africa, an indigenous conifer called yellowwood grows to heights near 180 feet and is a major source of lumber. In Australia and New Zealand, several species of conifers can be found amid the dominant and widespread eucalyptus forests.

Although true pines are not native to the Southern Hemisphere, they grow extremely well there. For instance, the radiata pine, which is native to Southern and Baja California, has been transplanted to South Africa, New Zealand, Australia and Chile. In its new locations, it has grown rapidly and extensively, becoming the most important pine species in all four countries.

Cone-bearing evergreens are by no means the only Southern Hemisphere evergreens. Far more common below the Equator are broad-leaved evergreens called sclerophyllous, a Greek word meaning "hard-leaved." Thriving in Mediterranean climates, where winters are typically warm and wet, these plants keep their leaves year round. Probably the best known are the eucalyptus trees, which account for more than 75 per cent of Australia's forests, but the group also includes evergreen oaks and beeches. Most abundant in Australia, South Africa and parts of Chile and Argentina, but also found around the Mediterranean Sea and in California, sclerophylls have small, leathery leaves that help to retain water through long, dry summers. During the summer, mature eucalyptus leaves hang vertically, reducing their exposure to the sun and minimizing water loss. As a result, both sides of the eucalyptus leaf support photosynthesis: Virtually all other broad leaves confine this food-producing capacity to the upper surface. Many eucalyptus trees were exported to California in the 19th Century and now flourish there, but broad-leaved evergreens cannot compete successfully with deciduous trees where the climate turns cold.

Just as many tree species are adapted to the environment found in certain ranges of latitude, so are they acclimated to particular altitudes. A vertical distance of only a few hundred feet can encompass a progression of tree types similar to patterns observed across several hundred miles of flatlands. In North America, the lower slopes of the northern Rocky Mountains are dominated by ponderosa pine and sugar pine. At an altitude of about 4,000 feet, the spires of Douglas fir and white fir begin to coarsen the texture of the forest canopy. The slender alpine firs start to appear above 9,000 feet, along with whitebark pine and Engelmann's spruce. These last, the so-called arctic spruces, inhabit the cruelest and coldest realms.

A different zonation characterizes the mountain slopes of different latitudes. In the Southern Rockies, sugar pine and ponderosa pine thrive at 6,000 feet, but they merge with Douglas fir and white fir at about 8,000 feet. Above these, near 10,000 feet, the slow-growing bristlecone pines find refuge in the inhospitable environment. Prisoners of the high altitude, these ancient trees are unable to evolve further or find another ecological niche. Gnarled and twisted, they seem to cling desperately to their age-old habitat in the rarefied mountain air.

The essential characteristic of the forests of the temperate latitudes is continuous change: Some of the most profound processes occur daily in the microscopic world of the individual tree cells; the most visible accompany

The changing seasons transform a section of
New Jersey beech forest in a pageant that
is played out each year in the broad-leaved
forests throughout the temperate zone.

WINTER

SPRING

SUMMER

FALL

111

the regular changing of the seasons; others overwhelm regions, even entire continents, as forests advance and retreat like a great green tide.

Over the millennia, adverse environmental changes have forced the forests to retreat many times, but as soon as conditions again became favorable, the trees started a long-range campaign to reclaim their lost territory. For example, near the eastern shore of Lake Michigan, as in many other parts of the world, forests stand where once there were lakes. No human lives long enough to see such a change come about, but scientists can read the story in its entirety by examining a succession of small lakes and ancient lake beds surrounding Lake Michigan.

When the last great ice age ended some 15,000 years ago, glacial meltwater enlarged the lake substantially. Eventually, as the waters receded, smaller ponds formed around the lake's perimeter. Cut off from the meltwater but still fed by streams, the sandy-bottomed ponds became catchments for rain water and attractive habitats for algae and other simple plants. Each of these basins then underwent a similar evolution. Over the years, the simple plants died and sank to the bottom, where their remains formed a layer of sediment. Airborne seeds of cattails and other pioneer plants drifted in to colonize the water's edge, and water lilies appeared in the deeper water near the center. In time, a dark, loamy humus accumulated on the bottom, until woody shrubs found sufficient soil to take root ever closer to the center of the pond, which was becoming a marsh. And among the shrubs were tree seedlings.

Elms, ashes and maples, which are tolerant of very damp soil, were the first to flourish at the edge of the marsh. They followed the shrubs toward the low-lying center, eventually turning the erstwhile pond into a swamp forest. The deciduous trees continued to grow taller and more dense, until their canopy closed over the struggling seedlings on the forest floor, reducing their chances of survival. Meanwhile, winds and animals were importing other kinds of seeds, including those of beech, oak, cherry, hickory and sugar maple—all of which are tolerant of shade. A few centuries later, the once-barren pond bottom was becoming a heterogeneous forest as different types of trees struggled for their place in the sun. Gradually, the beeches and sugar maples, which thrive in deep shade, gained hegemony over the ashes and elms. Even the oaks, cherries and hickories yielded to the dominant species. From time to time fire would course through the woods, exerting its unique influence on forest growth, but this was taken in stride by the survivors. Although many species endured in small numbers, the maples and beeches triumphed, and they will continue to predominate in this locale and climate until some unusual event forces a dramatic change.

This process of plant succession leading to a relatively steady state, or climax, is common to all forests. Different environments give rise to different types of climax communities. For example, farmland hewed out of a maple and beech forest will, if abandoned, eventually revert to the same type of forest. If the mountainous Douglas fir forests of Idaho burn down, aspens and other pioneers will move in for some 20 to 30 years, but eventually the great Douglas firs will reclaim their kingdom. Of course, since no forest ever comes to a developmental standstill, the triumph of one type of tree is always temporary, even if it is measured in centuries. The dominant species is typically surrounded by a host of other tree, shrub and herb species that offer stiff competition and are always ready to take advantage of

environmental change in the form of an altered climate, a flood, a plague of disease or insects, or human intervention.

The type of soil found in a region has a critical influence on the type of climax forest that will appear there. Many vegetation maps of Maryland, for example, suggest that most of its stable forests are dominated by oaks. And so they were at one time. But much of the original forest acreage has been destroyed by human activities, especially farming, and secondary forests have reclaimed half of the state, incorporating a wide variety of tree species. Because Maryland's climate is fairly uniform, and because there has been no significant climatic change during the last two centuries, it is clear that some other environmental factor has influenced forest patterns.

Maryland's topography consists of three distinct zones—the eastern coastal plain, the rich-soiled central Piedmont region and the Appalachian Mountains in the west. But according to a three-year study by Johns Hopkins University, these regional differences do not completely account for the variety of tree types found in the state. Predictably, white pine and eastern hemlock abound in the higher and colder mountain region, and bald cypress, which thrives in wetlands, populates some estuarine shores. But in the course of a stroll through the woods in the Appalachian area, a careful observer would note that the bear oaks—short, dark-limbed trees with rounded crowns—seem to appear and disappear from the land at random. They are often entirely absent only a short distance from glens where they abound. Just as suddenly, a trail in a coastal-plain forest may lead into stands of post, blackjack and chestnut oak, and from there into groves of willow oak and loblolly pine. Tulip poplars dominate areas in both the Piedmont and coastal plain, while sugar maple and basswood form distinct communities in the Appalachians. The abrupt changes are further complicated by the presence of certain saplings where no parent tree can be found.

Scientists began to understand this puzzling situation only after they had done some serious digging, focusing their efforts on Maryland's highly complex and varied geology. In some places the ground is underlain by limestone, in others by schist or shale, and the soils that accumulate on different kinds of bedrock have different characteristics. For example, the foundation of much of the Piedmont region consists of either igneous rocks such as granite, which are volcanic in origin, or metamorphic rocks such as gneiss, which are formed by intense heat and pressure. As these rocks decompose, they form very thick soils with a high capacity for water retention. But in the western part of the Piedmont the soil is derived from coarser-grained schist; it is thus more porous and retains relatively little water. After careful study of other variations in soil types, scientists have concluded that forest composition in Maryland has been determined more by the soil's ability to retain water than by elevation, latitude, soil chemistry, wind, fire or any other factor.

In young, open forests such as Maryland's, many kinds of trees grow into saplings. Few stands have yet formed the closed canopies under which shade and soil acidity can prevent the growth of a variety of trees. But by the time the trunks are about 10 inches in diameter, the moisture needs of different species become critical to further growth. Trees best suited to the moisture-retention capacity of the local soil survive; those less suited may adapt to the conditions or they may die. Thus, one might find chestnut oak, post oak, blackjack oak, willow oak and loblolly pine saplings in several areas. But if

Bright bands of autumn color mark the sequence of plant communities closing in on a dwindling bog in New York State. Each vegetative stage readies

the ground for the next in a process of forest succession that eventually will blanket the bog completely with mature forest.

the soil is sandy and low in water retention, the willow oaks and loblolly pines soon die out. On the other hand, these two trees will survive on more loamy soil, while the ranks of the others dwindle.

Because the dynamics of tree succession are almost universal, the same progression of forest patterns is found throughout the middle latitudes. In the absence of major environmental change, large trees such as beeches and oaks will eventually form a high canopy, while smaller trees—typically maples and birches—provide a secondary cover some 10 to 15 feet lower. Dogwoods, hollies and hawthorns eke out their existence beneath this second canopy. The resulting mixture of trees will shade the forest floor so thoroughly that few ground shrubs survive.

Homogeneous forests, such as the native oak forests of Maryland, at one time extended over most of North America east of the Mississippi, dominated in Northern areas by beech and sugar maples and in the South by oaks. But virgin forest is rarely found today anywhere in the temperate zone, even in the wilderness. One major reason is that deciduous trees thrive in precisely those climates that are best for agriculture. Trees were hacked down by the millions as generations of people cleared farmland, grazed animals and harvested fuel and building materials.

Humans are not the forest's only assailants. Insects, fungi and viruses attack from all directions, plunging into any open wound, consuming leaves, fruit and seeds, boring into bark, ensuring that no tree is ever at peace. But these pests and parasites have evolved with all forests and are an integral part of the ecosystem. Just as predatory wolf packs cull the cripples and the weaklings from a herd of caribou to the benefit of the herd, so do the many pestilences quickly kill unsuccessful trees, leaving more space and nourishment for stronger individuals and new generations.

At times, the balance of forces that creates and sustains the forest seems astonishingly delicate. The disappearance of some species of bird may allow harmful insects to gain the upper hand, or a slight change in regional rainfall may lead to the destruction of a tree species that has dominated a forest for centuries. However, for all the myriad creatures and events that can harm a forest, nothing since the Ice Age has altered the world's woodlands more drastically than human activity. Often, indirect and unintentional destruction has exceeded even the effects of the ax blade or the careless match, especially when human actions unleash some natural tree predator.

At the beginning of the 20th Century, millions of sturdy, towering chestnut trees provided luxuriant shade and excellent timber—as well as tasty nuts—throughout North America. In 1904, grounds keepers at New York City's Bronx Zoo noticed that one grove of chestnuts there seemed sickly. Within 10 months the trees were dead, within four years, thousands of the stately trees in the New York area had died, and it was obvious that the ailment was spreading westward. The chestnut blight, as it was called, was identified in 1906 as a fungus that had been imported accidentally from the Orient through the port of New York. By the 1930s, the deadly growth had annihilated virtually all mature chestnut trees in the United States.

About a decade after its arrival in North America, the blight appeared in Italy and in the early 1950s crossed the Alps into France. There the blight's progress was slowed when a French scientist developed a harmless fungus strain that is hardier than the lethal variety and often destroys it. Many infected trees have been saved by an injection of the harmless fungus into

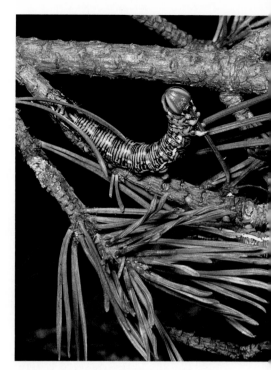

The caterpillar of a moth called the pine hawk, widespread in Europe, feasts on a pine needle. Forest damage ascribed to moths is in fact invariably the work of their voracious larvae; adult moths eat little or nothing and spend their few days of life mating and laying eggs.

Verdant forest is reduced to wintry desolation on a Pennsylvania hillside during a gypsy-moth infestation. A healthy forest will often produce a new mantle of leaves within a few weeks of losing its foliage to insects, but two consecutive years of defoliation will kill many trees.

their trunks, but even this imaginative defense has achieved only limited success. Many European trees still succumb to the fungus, and few North American chestnuts respond to the treatment. Scientists in Europe and the United States are trying to develop disease-resistant varieties by nurturing naturally resistant sprouts that grow from the stumps of infected trees. At the same time, researchers are trying to crossbreed North American chestnuts with an Asian variety that is naturally resistant to the fungus.

Similar devastation resulted when another fungus, first spotted in Europe by Dutch researchers in 1918, appeared in North American elm trees. Called Dutch elm disease, it is carried from tree to tree by elm bark beetles, and has wiped out millions of elm trees in the United States and Canada. Hybridization with disease-resistant Asian species yielded some promising results by the early 1980s, but no sure cure exists.

Although indigenous insects cause the most damage to North American forests, another immigrant, the gypsy moth, is one of the most notorious pests in wooded suburban areas. This insect was brought to Massachusetts from Europe by an entomologist who hoped to crossbreed it with silkworms to create a new silk-producing species. In 1869, about a dozen gypsy moth caterpillars escaped when a gust of wind blew open their cage. Once free, they bred prolifically. Voracious eaters, the creatures dine on virtually every kind of foliage, although their pattern of destruction indicates that they favor oak leaves. In little more than a century, these caterpillars have defoliated millions of trees throughout the Northeast, as far west as Michigan and as far south as Virginia, and their depredations continue.

Efforts to limit damage caused by these imported insects—as well as by native species—have been prodigious. Scientists have counterattacked with a variety of weapons, including potent pesticides, insect parasites, insect-eating birds, and even processed scents called pheromones, which lure insects into traps. An especially intriguing approach sets one insect against another. To fight the gypsy moth, for example, scientists breed and release wasps that prey upon the gypsy moth caterpillar. These wasps deposit their eggs on the skin of the caterpillar, and when the eggs hatch, the wasp larvae feed upon their hosts, killing them in the process. A biological weapon has also proved effective. Infested trees are sprayed with a solution containing bacteria that infect and eventually kill the caterpillars.

So complex is the forest ecosystem that sometimes efforts to prevent one type of calamity trigger another. In some areas of the American West, successful fire-prevention programs have allowed certain insect populations to grow unchecked and ravage trees as never before. Such setbacks make it increasingly clear that modern foresters need a profound understanding of the characteristics and dynamics of a wide variety of forests in order to provide effective forest management. At times, though, even the most sophisticated understanding and technique may not be enough.

One potentially serious threat to the forests of Europe and North America has only recently been recognized—air pollution. Industrial emissions of sulfur dioxide gas—the most abundant by-product of fossil-fuel combustion—have damaged many types of plants, including trees.

A highly controversial product of sulfur dioxide emission is acid rain—precipitation that has been made abnormally acid by chemical reaction with airborne pollutants. Acidity is measured by reference to the pH scale, which arbitrarily assigns the number seven to a substance that is neither acid nor alkaline. With each drop of a point on the scale, the acidity increases 10 times: A fluid with a pH of 5, for example, is 10 times more acid than one with a pH of 6. Ammonia, which is highly alkaline, has a pH of 12, baking soda has a pH of 8.2; vinegar has a pH of 3, lemon juice 1.8 and battery acid 1. Any precipitation with a pH lower than 5.6 is considered acid rain.

Some acid rain occurs naturally. In the Canadian Arctic, for example, exposed beds of lignite coal are sometimes ignited by lightning, and the ensuing fire can produce tremendous amounts of sulfur oxides. In early 1983, a huge acid cloud formed in the stratosphere at an altitude of about 100,000 feet after sulfurous dust was blasted aloft by the eruption of a Mexican volcano. These natural emissions combine with atmospheric moisture to form a mild sulfuric acid solution, which then falls to earth as acid rain or snow, typically with a pH near 4.5.

But a more insidious form of acid rain came to light near the end of the 19th Century, when the smokestacks that powered Europe's Industrial Revolution were belching tons of sulfurous material into the air each hour. Most people, basking in the unprecedented prosperity of the age, ignored the increasingly apparent effects of the fumes. Finally, in 1968, after so many decades of virtually unrestrained air pollution, a Swedish scientist named Svante Odén sounded a warning that was shrill enough to be heard above the industrial din. Declaring that acid rain was killing the wildlife in hundreds of Scandinavian lakes, Odén publicly accused Germany and England of waging a kind of chemical warfare against his country. Odén's alarming language caught the attention of the press, and soon the problem of acid rain became a worldwide concern. Subsequent studies on the seemingly pristine Greenland icecap have shown that acid deposits in that area have been rising since the beginning of the Industrial Age.

The most obvious effect of acid rain is its ability to kill fish in lakes and streams. When their gills are irritated by the acidity, and certain metals are leached out of the soil by the acid water, the fish secrete a protective film of mucus over their delicate gill tissues. If the acidity becomes too great or if it is prolonged, the mucus clogs the gills and the fish die. In Scandinavia, Canada and the Northeastern United States, hundreds of lakes that once teemed with fish have been left virtually lifeless by acid rain.

Plastic collars loop around tree trunks to collect trickling rain water for a West German study of acid rain. Tainted rain filtering through the forest canopy may collect additional toxic chemicals that have been deposited on bark and foliage by polluted air.

During the last decade, some studies have blamed extensive forest damage on acid rain. Forests located near industrial centers in Central Europe seem to be the hardest hit. In West Germany, it is believed by some researchers that during a recent five-year period, acid rain killed about 3,750 acres of woodland and seriously damaged another 200,000 acres. According to West German biochemist and acid rain specialist Bernhard Ulrich, the most vulnerable forests are dense stands of conifers that are between 20 and 40 years old. Ulrich believes that these trees in West Germany will have only limited growth, and that the effects on the soil may be irreversible.

According to Ulrich's hypothesis, the damage done to forests by acid rain occurs in four phases. In phase one, the nitrogen and sulfur compounds that account for the acidity of the precipitation actually fertilize the soil, causing the trees to grow faster for a time. Most soils, particularly those that are rich in alkaline limestone, have the capacity to neutralize some acid. But this is a limited defense, and Ulrich finds that the cumulative effects of many years of continued acid deposition impair the soil's neutralizing capacity. In the next phase, sulfates combine with calcium, magnesium and other nutrients and leach them from the soil. The resulting deficiency causes pine needles, for example, to turn yellow.

In phase three of Ulrich's scenario, sulfates begin to combine with metals in the soil. Aluminum is present in large quantities in most soils, but usually it is bound to organic compounds and is essentially harmless. However, when the acid breaks up these compounds and releases the aluminum, the ubiquitous metal becomes highly toxic. Typically, this occurs when the soil pH is 4.2. And when the amount of toxic aluminum exceeds the amount of calcium in the soil, the tops of the trees growing in it begin to die. Then the aluminum intensifies the attack. Coming in contact with the fine roots and root hairs, the aluminum prevents cell division, interferes with the roots' ability to transport water, and impairs the trees' defense systems, making them more vulnerable to insects and diseases. Thus weakened, the trees are also more susceptible to injury caused by other natural stresses, such as cold and drought. Ulrich thinks that in the fourth and final phase, which has not yet been observed in large areas, the trees may succumb to a combination of starvation, disease and poisoning. By 1982, according to Ulrich, some 5 million acres of German forest soils were on the threshold of phase three.

The problem has serious international implications because pollution from one country may cause acid rain to fall on another. The great concentration of industrial activity on the Rhine and the Ruhr Rivers affects most of Central Europe, and the Soviet Union, which suffers somewhat from the European emissions, is itself sending fumes into Finland. In North America, acid rain falls on roughly half of the continent as a result of the tremendous number of fossil fuel-burning utilities and metal-smelting plants in the industrialized Midwestern areas in the United States and Canada.

There can be no doubt that 20th Century civilization has had a profound and largely negative effect on the world's temperate forests. Nonetheless, the forests have demonstrated many times over their ability to survive even extraordinary adversity. It would be foolish to underestimate the danger to forests that is posed by modern industrial society, but because change and adaptation are the woodlands' greatest strength, it is still too soon to foresee an end to the great sylvan choreography of the temperate latitudes. Ω

Chapter 5

TACTICS FOR THE TROPICS

In 1970, the government of Brazil was facing staggering social and economic problems. A disastrous drought had driven 10 per cent of the country's population from their farms, and 30 million destitute people were struggling to stay alive, many of them jammed into urban slums along the northeast coast. But officials thought they saw a solution. As a means of providing the displaced farmers with land and a livelihood, the Brazilian government conceived of an audacious assault on the largest rain forest in the world.

The jungle region known as Amazonia, the basin of the 4,080-mile Amazon River and its tributaries, covers more than two million square miles in six South American countries. It is one of the most forbidding areas on earth and, although a few mysterious and elusive tribes make their home there, has repeatedly rebuffed colonizing attempts. Still, its spaces have never ceased to exercise a powerful allure, and Brazil's maladies now added weight to the conquering urge. The rallying cry was "Land with no men for men with no land."

The government's strategy was to bulldoze a 1,980-mile-long path straight through the luxuriant green heart of Amazonia; the dirt road would be christened, rather grandly, the Transamazon Highway. The planners envisioned that, with travel to the interior made possible, as many as one million people could be moved into the area by 1980 and settled on 250-acre farms that would be carved out of the rain forest along the highway. In addition, the road would provide access to the area's rich mineral deposits and wealth of timber.

The jungle threw up prodigious obstacles to this dream. The road-building work force of 11,000 men lived for months at a time in camps so remote that food and supplies had to be dropped to them by airplane. They labored in heat of 90° F. and more, constant high humidity, drenching downpours and plagues of insects that burrowed beneath clothes and dug into the flesh, bringing malaria and various other fevers. As the work progressed, flaws in the planning and research done for the project became increasingly evident. Rivers were found meandering 20 miles from where the mapmakers had thought they were; hills rose defiantly where the charts showed flat land.

As bad as conditions were for the workers, the project visited even worse miseries on the resident Indian tribes. The intrusion of 20th Century civilization into the rain forest brought with it deadly infections of measles, influenza and whooping cough, along with social disruption that resulted in

Nurtured by perpetual mists, a cloud forest of vines, gnarled trees, ferns and mosses flourishes on an Ecuadorian mountainside. Cloud forests are one of 13 recognizable types of tropical rain forest, determined by different altitudes, amounts of rainfall and soil conditions.

alcoholism and prostitution among the jungle people. By the time construction was completed in 1975, increasingly disillusioned Brazilians were calling the Transamazon Highway the Transamargura—the highway of bitterness.

Formidable problems also beset the government's relocation efforts, which began in 1971. Settlers trying to farm the cleared land along the highway found their jungle environment to be anything but hospitable. Malaria, previously unknown in Amazonia but brought in by the first new residents, rapidly took on epidemic proportions; the bulldozing of the natural landscape had created innumerable pools of water in which the disease-carrying Anopheles mosquito multiplied. Even worse, the seasonal epidemics of malaria tended to peak during the planting and harvest times, when farmers most needed to be able to tend their fields.

Crop yields were poor from the outset and soon decreased. The strains of rice recommended to the settlers by government advisers failed to produce in the thin rain-forest soil. Moreover, the soil lost what nutrients it had after two or three years of exposure to sun and rain. At the same time, the highway itself fell victim to the elements; large sections of dirt road, lacking the protective canopy and anchoring roots of the native forest, washed away during the frequent downpours.

The utilization of Amazonia's raw materials proved to be similarly disappointing. Apart from the output of one tin mine, the mineral riches were not forthcoming. Eight small and remote lumber mills processed commercially valuable trees, such as mahogany and tropical cedar, that were found near the highway, but the high cost of transportation made the harvesting of trees from deep within the jungle unprofitable.

By 1981, the signs of failure were undeniable. Instead of the contemplated one million settlers, a mere 57,000 people had relocated to the humid valleys along the Transamazon Highway—and 60 per cent of them had packed up and left. Scientists and naturalists, who had criticized the project from the outset, blamed the expensive fiasco on the Brazilian government's failure to understand that the rain forest is something of a counterfeit paradise.

Tropical rain forests, the largest of which is Brazil's jungle, are found in a narrow belt that girdles the globe at the Equator. In this region the sun, rising high in the sky throughout the year, maintains relatively constant average annual temperatures of between 68° and 82° F., and annual rainfall of more than 70 inches on the average is distributed fairly evenly all year round. Tropical rain forests occur in West Africa as far north as Zaire, from the Indian subcontinent into Malaysia, in a narrow strip of eastern Australia, over most of New Guinea, and through extensive regions of Central and South America (*map, page 104*).

Nowhere else on earth is biological productivity and diversity so evident as in the tropical forest. Scientists believe that about two thirds of the earth's estimated 4.5 million plant and animal species dwell in this warm, damp environment. As many as 100 different species of plants may twine around the trunk or cling to the leafy crown of a single rain-forest tree. One tenth of all the bird species in the world live in the Amazon forest, and some 2,500 types of fish populate the Amazon River. The Amazon basin shelters 150 bat species, 54 types of nutmeg, tapirs weighing 450 pounds, violets 25 feet high, 250-pound catfish, and tarantulas so huge that they snare birds for dinner. Yet fewer than one in six of the species thought to exist in the jungle have actually been found.

The lure of gold and cinnamon—a highly prized spice—attracted the first European adventurers to Amazonia in 1541. A party of 60 Spaniards, led by a brutal military commander named Francisco de Orellana, traveled the length of the Amazon from the Andes to the river's mouth. The size of the river and the number of lesser streams feeding into it moved de Orellana to write, "It is a maze that only God can figure out."

The journey took 17 months, far longer than the party had expected or provided for. Supplies ran out long before they reached the sea, and they began raiding Indian villages for food. They were forced to eat toads and snakes and eventually to devour their leather belts and shoes, boiled in an herb broth, to stay alive. They were attacked frequently by Indians, and they also reported an encounter with a group of white female warriors. Friar Gaspar de Carvajal, whose journal provides the only record of the harrowing journey, described the women as "very white and tall, having their hair long and braided and wound about their heads, and they are very robust and go about naked." The Spaniards called these remarkable women Amazons, after the female warriors of Greek mythology. No such women were ever seen by anyone else, but the tale provided the name for the world's second-longest river (the Nile, just 60 miles longer than the Amazon, is the record holder).

Nearly 100 years later, a Portuguese expedition of 2,000 men and 47 boats managed to travel from the mouth of the Amazon upstream to map the interior. But another 200 years passed before the first scientific reconnaissance of the region was made. This was the accomplishment of a brilliant French mathematician and geographer named Charles Marie de la

The Transamazon Highway—traced on this map—snakes 1,980 miles through the heart of the world's largest tropical rain forest. Completed in 1975, the highway failed to stimulate the hoped-for settlement of the region and remains little used.

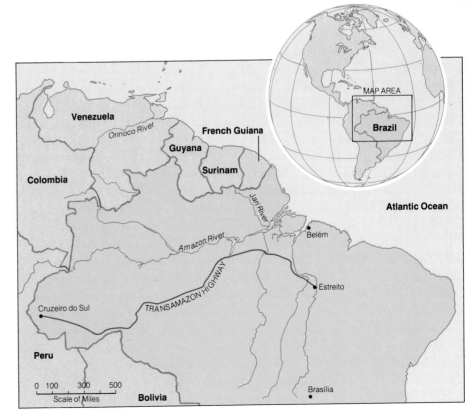

Condamine. During a two-month journey down the Amazon, he recorded the depth and rate of flow of the river and collected botanical specimens. He also noted that the sap of certain plants had some most unusual properties: Indians had been using it for centuries to fashion bouncing balls, and more recently they had devised crude waterproof boots with it. La Condamine took some of the pliable gum back to Europe, where the eminent English scientist Joseph Priestley, whose experiments would lay the foundations of modern chemistry, found a new application: He discovered that it was capable of rubbing out pencil marks. Priestley named the remarkable stuff rubber.

The substance remained of limited usefulness until 1839, when a failed American businessman named Charles Goodyear accidentally dropped some rubber mixed with sulfur on a hot stove and thus perfected a process he had been working on for years. Called vulcanization, it made raw rubber stronger, harder and more durable. Applications for the improved material burgeoned, and soon a substantial sap-harvesting industry had emerged to satisfy world demand for waterproof fabrics, elastic bands, hoses, boots and tires—first for bicycles, later for automobiles.

Because the harvest from Brazil's native rubber trees could not keep pace with the worldwide appetite, attempts were made to cultivate rubber trees on plantations, but the proximity of the cultivated trees made them susceptible to epidemics of a native leaf blight, and the plantings were wiped out. Predictably, entrepreneurs began to wonder if cultivation was possible elsewhere. In 1876, an English coffee planter named Henry Wickham sent a shipment of rubber-tree seeds to London, where they were germinated in a greenhouse. About 1,900 seedlings were then shipped to Ceylon, Singapore and Java. They flourished so prodigiously in rain-forest plantations that Brazil was relegated to a minor role as a source of raw rubber. For his part in the global restructuring of a basic industry, Wickham received a knighthood.

Meanwhile, the early European explorers had been returning from the Amazonian wilderness with dazzling descriptions of its lushness and had introduced to their homelands other riches of the rain forest: valuable hardwoods such as mahogany, various fruits and nuts, and medicinal plants. In their quest to wrest fortunes from the jungle, most Europeans despoiled their surroundings. They also enslaved or killed many Indians. But two self-taught English naturalists, Alfred Russel Wallace and Henry Bates, brought different sensibilities to the rain forest in 1848 when they came in search of specimens instead of spoils. The pair spent a year acclimating themselves in the small port city of Belém before embarking on an expedition to collect samples of plant and animal life to take back to European museums.

Wallace and Bates were entranced by the lush vistas of the rain forest. A great canopy of green towered overhead, forming a vault like that of a cathedral. The interwoven, mushroom-shaped tops of the trees—some of them more than 120 feet tall—kept all but 1 per cent of the sunlight from reaching the ground. As a result, the forest floor was largely bare, but climbing vines and other plants managed to get a substantial share of the sun's energy. "Some were twisted in strands like cables," Bates wrote later, "others had thick stems contorted in every variety of shape, entwining snakelike round the tree trunks or forming gigantic loops and coils among

Along a stretch of the Transamazon Highway, rainy-season downpours have stripped away the thin soil to expose the hard red clay beneath. Only a small fraction of the highway is paved, and much of the route has fallen into disuse.

the larger branches; others, again, were of zigzag shape, or indented like the steps of a staircase, sweeping from the ground to a giddy height."

After four years in the Amazon rain forest, Wallace sailed for home with a collection of live monkeys, macaws, parrots and parakeets, plus a sizable number of preserved specimens. He was certain that his finds would astonish the scientific community, but his triumph was marred by disaster. Three weeks into the voyage home, his ship caught fire. Wallace and the crew escaped on a lifeboat, from which they were rescued after drifting for eight days, but his entire collection was lost. Nonetheless, Wallace was hailed for his achievements in Amazonia and, later, as a pioneer—along with Charles Darwin—of the theory of evolution.

Bates, meanwhile, stayed on in Amazonia for another seven years, finally returning to Britain with specimens of 14,712 animal species, 8,000 of which were new to science. The remarkable defense technique of certain butterfly species that imitate dangerous or foul-tasting creatures was first described by Bates, and is now known as Batesian mimicry.

The obvious biological voluptuousness that dazzled the first investigators convinced naturalists that the soil beneath the forest would surely yield similarly bountiful crops. It took a great deal of study and painful experience to bring to light a remarkable paradox; the rain forest's ecological productivity is perpetuated on nutritionally bankrupt soil.

Amazonia has not always been the site of a dense green jungle. Thirty million years ago, a long dry period decimated the area's tropical rain forests, leaving only isolated pockets of jungle surrounded by wide expanses of grassland. Each of the remaining pockets pursued its own evolutionary course, its myriad species adapting in various ways. Thus when climatic conditions changed many thousands of years later, allowing the forests to spread out again and rejoin, each pocket contributed different species to the resulting mix. As a consequence, the South American forests are among the most diverse in the world. While four or five tree species may be found in a few square miles of temperate forest, several hundred species may populate the same area of rain forest. Extensive stands of a single kind of tree abound in a temperate forest, but such collections are rare in the crowded rain forest, where it is often necessary to travel a mile from one tree to find another of the same species.

Leaf fall occurs continuously and slowly in the rain forest, unlike the sudden annual drop of deciduous trees, and in the tropical heat and moisture the leaves decompose rapidly. Therefore, the humus that enriches the soil of more temperate latitudes does not have a chance to accumulate in the jungle. After millions of years of daily rainfall and constant heat, the unreplenished soil has been leached of much of its nutrient content, leaving it rich in aluminum and iron oxides. These chemicals impart a telltale red color to the earth and make it highly acidic, a property that is destructive of the few nutrients that remain. In fact, when a section of the forest is burned over and cleared for farming, the only nutrients available in the soil are usually those in the ashes, and they are soon lost to erosion, leaching and harvests.

The ecosystem of a tropical rain forest is, in a sense, upside down by comparison with that of a temperate forest: Its nutrients are stored not in the soil, as is usual farther north or south, but overhead in the canopy. In

Marvels of Deception

In the intensely competitive world of a rain forest, many small creatures use mimicry to enhance their chances of survival. Some harmless animals mimic dangerous ones to discourage predators. The coloring of a number of snake species resembles that of the poisonous coral snake. Other creatures have developed coloration that blends with their surroundings: The transparent wings of a glasswing butterfly are almost invisible, and the mottled skin of one kind of frog resembles bird droppings. Still others have adapted their behavior to support their deception; some katydids sway in the breeze like the leaves they are imitating, and twig caterpillars fall stiffly to the ground if dislodged.

Scientists do not know how such creatures select locations appropriate to their camouflage. Some experiments indicate that their primitive brains may contain a genetic imprint that impels the animal to keep moving until it finds itself in a setting that makes the best use of its evolutionary strategy.

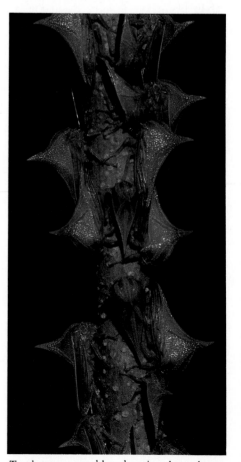

Tree hoppers resemble a daunting thorn cluster.

Mottled colors, veining and projecting eye hoods disguise an Asiatic horned frog resting on dead leaves.

Shade variations add realism to three leaf-mimicking katydids.

A mantid all but disappears against a gray tree trunk.

A gliding gecko of Southeast Asia rests on a gnarled branch.

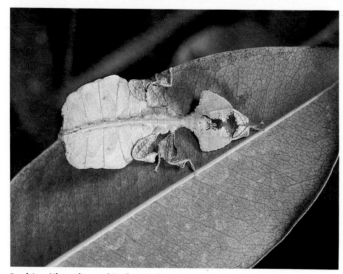

Looking like a decayed leaf, an Indonesian mantid awaits prey.

Emerald green coloration helps camouflage a Mulu lizard.

Moths native to Costa Rica blend with a lichen-covered branch.

A defenseless caterpillar masquerades as a green parrot vine snake.

A bush cricket in Costa Rica protects itself by duplicating the color and texture of a moss-cloaked leaf.

the vigorous competition for light and space in the tropics, trees evolved long, slender trunks, with most branching and leafing activity concentrated in the crowns. The canopy formed by the spherical crowns is so dense that rain water from a driving tropical downpour may not reach the ground for 10 minutes after it has drenched the rain-forest roof.

The canopy is further knitted together by woody vines that creep up the trees from the forest floor to explode in a burst of green when they attain the light of the sun. Then they continue to snake through the treetops, sometimes reaching a length of 300 feet or more. Other plants, called epiphytes—a group that includes orchids, ferns, bromeliads and even cacti—have no connection to the ground at all. They are rooted on high branches, where they draw nutrients from rain water, from windblown debris and from decaying vegetation that constantly sifts downward from taller trees and forms a thick layer of humus on wide branches below. This shower of detritus is so rich that some rain-forest trees send out a type of aerial root to partake of the feast.

Some equally ingenious adaptations are seen among the flowers and leaves of trees. In one adaptation, called cauliflory, the flowers emerge and bloom directly from the trunk, where they are less likely to be obscured by the canopy vegetation and are more available for pollination by passing birds, insects and bats. Leaves represent a major investment of scarce nutrients, and those of most tropical trees contain a toxin capable of sickening leaf-eating mammals and insects. Curare, the deadly poison used on arrow tips by some tribes (and in small doses by doctors as a muscle relaxant), is a toxin found in the leaves of a number of plant species. The animal kingdom, of course, can adapt too. In an example of the constant action-reaction of evolution, the South American tapir, a browsing piglike animal, has learned to eat only a few leaves from one plant before moving on to another, thus ensuring that it never ingests enough of any one toxin to upset its digestive system.

In the rich tangle of leaves, branches, roots and vines aloft, many forest animals and insects live their entire lives, never descending to the ground. The tree sloth, for example, has powerful, specialized claws that enable it to hang indefinitely from a tree limb but make walking all but impossible. Mice and ants skitter among the leaves, and earthworms burrow into humus collected on branches 90 feet high. Water accumulates in the cuplike bases of a number of bromeliads, creating a microhabitat populated by worms, mosquito larvae, young frogs, dragonflies and even a species of crab.

From its lofty foundation, the rain-forest food chain extends both upward and downward. Swifts swoop over the canopy, seeking such small prey as the residents of the bromeliads; and eagles wheel on high, looking for the monkeys that swing through the trees in search of fruit. On the ground below, snakes flourish, feeding on the multitudes of frogs and lizards. Here, too, competition has resulted in notable examples of specialization. One bird species eats only insects driven up from the ground by army ants; its droppings provide food for a certain species of butterfly. But except for panthers and some other cats, few large carnivores live in the perpetual twilight of the forest floor; there is little there for them to eat.

While most of the resources of the rain forest are concentrated about 100 feet above the ground, the height of most trees, a few scattered giants rise to 200 feet or more. Because these skyscrapers soar above the main

Having cleared land by felling trees and burning them after they dried, members of Borneo's Dyak tribe plant rice seeds amid the nourishing ashes. When slash-and-burn agriculture is used on poor soils, nutrients quickly leach away. After a few years of harvests, the clearing must be abandoned and new areas burned and planted.

canopy and thus do not benefit from its stabilizing effect, they often have great buttressing roots that help to anchor them to a broad base of soil. The flanged roots may emerge as high as 30 feet up the trunk, yet reach less than two feet into the soil. The protrusive root network also traps detritus and silt, providing additional nourishment for the tree.

Beneath the canopy, an understory of trees manages to thrive despite the dense shade. Saplings often grow to about 12 feet in height, then stop, enduring sometimes for years until a tree falls and creates an opening in the canopy. Spurred by the sudden shaft of sunlight, the understory flora surges upward to drink in the light and rapidly fill the void.

To fell this rain-forest tree, a logger must first slice through its enormous buttress roots. The formations distribute the weight of a shallow-rooted tree and help to prevent it from toppling in strong winds.

The fall of a giant tree rends the fabric of the canopy and instantly alters the web of life that it had supported. For those who witness such an occurrence, it is impressive indeed. In 1962, a young English anthropologist, Vernon Reynolds, reported from the Budongo forest in Uganda: "Every few days I hear a giant crash, and I can tell the distance by whether it is like a cannon or just a dull thud, and whether the ground trembles. That a huge tree, so many tons of timber, which has struggled toward the light, grown broad and spread its branches wide against its neighbors, fruited season after season and fed hundreds of generations of birds and monkeys, drained the soil of its goodness and enriched it with decaying leaves, given shade and fodder to elephants, and provided life for a million insects, that this piece of the structure of the living earth should crash down with unbelievable destruction from its firm unshakable vertical is an event of such enormity and yet such insignificance that I cannot comprehend it."

Rain forests are not the only type of forest found in the tropics. An annual dry spell lasting a few months accounts for the very different ecology of the *cerradao* of Brazil, the "dry evergreen" forests in West Africa and the monsoon forests of Indo-Malaysia. Trees in these forests are generally shorter than those of the rain forest, and in many cases their bark is thicker, to provide protection against dryness. Buttresses are uncommon, and moisture-loving epiphytes cannot survive. Such forests are semideciduous:

The brilliant red color of the ripe fruit on a lowland rain-forest shrub serves to catch the eye of hungry animals. When the fruit is devoured, the seeds inside pass unharmed through the animal's digestive tract and often take root far from the parent plant.

The round, woody fruit of the cannonball tree takes 30 months to ripen and fall. The seeds inside are at last released to germinate only after the tough shells have disintegrated.

The lower stories are evergreen, but the canopy sheds its leaves in the dry season, often flowering soon afterward. The leaves return before the rainy season begins. In places such as West Africa, where there is a longer annual dry spell, all the trees shed their leaves.

In areas of prolonged dryness and no predictable rainy season, the trees are shorter still, more thorny than leafy, and ultimately give way to savanna, such as the great grasslands of East Africa. Where the rain forest nears the sea or a river estuary with its salty water, the forest stops. Its species cannot tolerate salt, even in the atmosphere. If the shoreline is relatively sandy, the rain forest gives way to palm trees, as in some Caribbean islands; if the shore is muddy—as it is in parts of Southeast Asia—the trees that reach forth toward the water are mangroves, a unique and stabilizing tangle that fights tidal erosion and reclaims land from the water.

The first trees to colonize such an area are low, shrubby mangrove species that are uniquely equipped to anchor themselves to the shifting bottom and survive regular inundation by salty tidal water. Their long, pyramid-shaped roots reach into the muddy floor, where oxygen is extremely scarce, and send shoots upward to absorb oxygen from the air to fill the needs of the roots below. The thick, fleshy leaves absorb and release excess salt collected from the trees' water supply.

Silt builds up among the mass of roots, and the short mangroves edge ever farther out. Meanwhile, others—usually taller and less able to withstand prolonged inundation—move in behind, forming a great swampy forest that supports a host of birds and animals. Mangrove forests also provide shelter for marine organisms such as oysters and crabs, which find protection and rich food supplies in the dense, matted, silty zone that is half sea, half land.

The high-altitude rain forests that flourish in such areas as the mountains of Malaysia, New Guinea, and Central and South America are even more diverse, but somewhat less vigorous, than the lowland tropical rain forest. With every thousand feet of additional altitude, temperature drops about 4 degrees, retarding the rate of photosynthesis in leaves and therefore slowing the other metabolic activities of the plant. Diversity, however, increases with altitude up to about 8,000 feet, partly because the ecosystem is less stable than that of the lowland forests; landslides, for instance, frequently open areas of the forest to pioneer growth.

Where the land is almost permanently shrouded in moisture-laden clouds—at altitudes as low as 3,000 feet in some mountainous areas of tropical islands—the forest assumes yet another aspect. Here the air is damp and cool, and plants lost in the almost continuous fog of the so-called cloud forest tend to be covered with moss or festooned with epiphytes, their leaves often leathery and small. One such cloud forest clinging to the mountains of Kauai, one of the westernmost and oldest of the volcanic formations of Hawaii, is perhaps the wettest spot on earth: Annual rainfall averages 486 inches, or more than 40 feet. The wildlife population of cloud forests is abundant but far less diverse than in the lowland forests, which may well have given rise to the human species itself.

Human ancestors probably first emerged from the tropical rain forest some 12 million years ago to populate open savannas, where competition was less intense. Today, fewer than a million people subsist as hunter-gatherers deep in the rain forest; a number of tribes can be found along Amazonia's network of rivers; New Guinea's rain forests support a few isolated tribes, as do the rain forests of Indo-Malaysia.

But with dismaying speed, such cultures are disappearing. Ninety-six Amazonian tribes have vanished since 1900, most of them victims of disease introduced by outsiders. In addition, bitter prejudice has contributed to the abuse or murder of forest Indians, especially those of Brazil. Indians there have been machine-gunned, given sugar laced with arsenic or forced into servitude. Despite an apparent end to such atrocities, the forest tribes' contact with civilization still brings death in the form of disease.

A few forest tribes continue to live in much the same way as countless generations of their ancestors, and others have made compromises with modern civilization. Around the edges of the Ituri Forest of Zaire, a variety of tribes make their living by growing manioc, a root crop similar to the sweet potato, in patches of cleared land. For them, the forest is both a natural and supernatural menace. The soil exhausts itself after about three years, forcing the villagers to pack up their belongings and move to another site and go through the exhausting business of cutting down another tract of huge trees. The forest contains leopards that can carry off livestock, and elephants that can trample garden plots. The villagers practice witchcraft to ward off the forest's palpable hostility.

Occasionally, small bands of Pygmies known as the Mbuti visit these hot, dusty villages. The Pygmies normally live deep in the forest, but they emerge from time to time to enjoy the relative ease of village life. The villagers treat the Mbuti as a subclass and constantly seek to persuade them to take up proper lives in the villages. But the Mbuti soon tire of living among the more settled villagers and return to their forest home. Theirs is a friendly, humorous, even joyous culture in which the forest is the benevolent provider of a year-round supply of game and anything else they truly need. "It is not surprising," wrote British anthropologist Colin Turnbull, who spent years among both groups, "that the Mbuti recognize their dependence upon the forest and refer to it as 'Father' or 'Mother.' As they say, it gives them food, warmth, shelter and clothing just like their parents. What is, perhaps, surprising is that the Mbuti add that the forest also, like their parents, gives them affection."

Civilized people seem, like the village tribes, bent on combating the rain forest rather than living with it. In the case of Brazil's construction of the Transamazon Highway, planners attempted to impose conditions on a forest system they had not first studied. As tropical biologist Peter Raven, an ardent spokesman for scientists' concern about destruction of rain forests, said of the Amazon project after it was under way: "Hopes are pinned on manipulating a system in which only somewhat over half of the elements have been registered, much less understood. Imagine trying to build a computer or an airplane from such a starting point!"

Similar lack of knowledge is not hindering the decimation of tropical rain forests worldwide. In the last 100 years, the world's supply of tropical rain forests has been cut in half; every hour, some scientists estimate, another 400 acres are cleared. The National Research Council's Committee on Research Priorities in Tropical Biology, chaired by Raven, predicted in 1980 that by the year 2000 the only tropical rain forests remaining untouched will be in western Amazonia and in Zaire.

Securely tethered to a rope network, biologist Donald Perry examines a spiky-leaved bromeliad 110 feet above the jungle floor. Branches in the canopy are normally encrusted with a rich variety of plants, but the limb on which Perry sits has been worn bare by his travels along it.

With an ingenious system of ropes reminiscent of a spider's web, tropical biologist Donald Perry has studied the canopy of a rain forest from unprecedented points of view. Some biologists have used stationary observation platforms in canopy trees, but Perry found them too confining. On a 1979 expedition to Costa Rica, he developed a lofty rigging that enabled him to perch on tree limbs or dangle in space, observing plants and animals without obstruction from the dense understory foliage.

At the Finca La Selva research station of the Organization for Tropical Studies in Costa Rica, Perry enclosed about two thirds of an acre of jungle with a triangle of strong, lightweight nylon rope strung more than a hundred feet above the ground. Strapped into a safety harness attached to a pulley, he propelled himself along the rope triangle and raised and lowered himself on a vertical rope to make observations at different levels. Perry's forays even took him downward into the dark confines of a 120-foot-tall hollow tree, where he found a habitat teeming with spiders, centipedes, bats, scorpions and three-inch-long cockroaches.

Insects flying up into a net trap are funneled into a collecting jar containing cyanide. Perry placed four traps at different levels of the forest; this one alone ensnared more than 10,000 different kinds of insects.

A tree frog rests on an orchid plant in the upper canopy. Many such frogs lay their eggs aloft in rain water trapped in cup-shaped blossoms; this species is thought to clamber down to the ground to lay its eggs in ponds.

Camouflage makes the great potoo almost indistinguishable from its lichen-covered roost. A nocturnal hunter of the canopy top, the bird is so seldom seen that Perry was the first person to photograph it in its natural habitat.

Strange Denizens of Tropical Trees

A vertical section of the rain forest is a series of overlapping habitats, each characterized by a particular mix of animals and plants. In terms of numbers of life forms, the richest zone is the canopy top, where intense sunlight fosters lush vegetation that supports a teeming animal population. The animals adapted to the high reaches are seldom found at ground level. Of the 80 species of bees Donald Perry has collected at Finca La Selva, some are the principal pollinators of only the tallest trees, while others, such as golden bees, are generally found only at the lower levels. The high-level bee varieties were once thought rare, but Perry's collections in previously inaccessible spots prove that they are plentiful. Even mosquitoes sort themselves out, with the stronger species rising to the top to bedevil the resident monkeys—and infect them with yellow fever.

A lethal fungus sprouts like antlers from the head of its victim, a bullet ant. Unlike most rain-forest insects, this ant species forages from the bottom of the forest to the top.

In the gloomy light near the floor of the forest, an ogre-faced spider suspended by a slender thread captures its prey in an unconventional web it holds with six of its legs.

Donald Perry lowers himself into a hollow tree that houses a colony of bats *(bottom)*. The bat guano that accumulates in the cavelike chamber probably serves the tree as fertilizer.

The legendary languor of its movements and the greenish tint of its fur (due to growths of algae) make the three-toed sloth hard to spot in the forest's shadowy middle level.

Scientists have just begun to calculate the price of such a loss. The constant cycling of water through rain and evaporation contributes several thousand gallons of water to the atmosphere per acre of rain forest each day, with the result that over half of the earth's water vapor exists in the humid tropics. Furthermore, removal of the rain forests' demand for carbon dioxide could elevate the amount of the gas in the atmosphere and thus contribute to a global warming trend. More subtly felt would be the consequences for medicine. About 45 per cent of all prescription drugs contain ingredients originating in the flora of the rain forest. Medication to treat leukemia is derived from the rosy periwinkle, a trailing plant that grows in Madagascar. Steroids for contraceptives, and L-dopa, used in treating Parkinson's disease, originate in the rain forest.

The search continues for new botanical miracle drugs, and scientists believe that the jungles contain more than a million as yet unidentified plant species; invaluable pharmaceuticals may well be discovered within that remarkable diversity.

New food crops also might be found among those unidentified plants: Most of the handful of grains that now feed the world, including corn, wheat and rice, originated in the tropics. And a recent discovery there—a form of wild maize, the ancestor of modern corn, that is a virus-resistant perennial—offers new hope for hungry populations.

The relentless destruction of the tropical rain forests recalls the belief among a tribe of South American Indians that the trees of the forest hold up the sky. According to the ancient legend of the very people who were the first to suffer the intrusion of civilization into the forest, the fall of the trees will precipitate the downfall of the earth. Ω

AN ILL-FATED FOREST EMPIRE

When the reclusive American billionaire Daniel K. Ludwig foresaw a worldwide paper shortage looming in the 1960s, he was determined to profit from it on a colossal scale. In 1967, he purchased more than four million acres of tropical rain forest along Brazil's Jari River, a tributary of the Amazon, 250 miles inland from the coastal port city of Belém. And from that isolated stretch of Amazonian jungle he began to carve a forest-products empire.

Ludwig invested one billion dollars to create the Jari Forest and Agricultural Company. A pulp mill and power plant were assembled in Japan, then towed to Jari on two enormous barges. He constructed housing for 30,000 people in four jungle towns, complete with a hospital and schools. Ludwig's private air fleet, operating out of three airports on the property, provided air-shuttle service to and from the remote development. Goods and equipment were moved around the project on 2,800 miles of private roads and 26 miles of railway. More than 500 cars and trucks and countless pieces of heavy machinery were imported, along with more than 266 mechanics to keep them running.

But by the mid-1970s, despite the massive infusion of capital, the world's largest tropical tree farm—and largest privately owned piece of land—faced serious and unexpected problems.

Under tow in Japan's Inland Sea *(above)*, the paper-pulp plant embarks on a journey of 15,500 miles to Daniel K. Ludwig's massive forest-products project on the Jari River, deep in the Brazilian rain forest. The plant—shown in place at right—was designed to process trees into 800 tons of pulp every day.

Clearing the Forest for the Trees

The remarkable diversity of the dense natural forest native to the Jari region made its destruction a prerequisite of Ludwig's audacious pulpwood project. Of the more than 300 different tree species per acre that flourished there, most were either unwanted or impossible to harvest profitably; markets existed for only a few hardwoods. So the jungle had to be cleared to make way for the cultivation of suitable trees. While some of the native lumber was salvaged for building materials and fuel, most of it was burned in fires so immense that the updrafts spawned thunderstorms six miles away.

In clearing the land, Jari's foresters quickly discovered the astonishing fragility of the soil. "Jungle crushers," enormous bulldozers brought in to tear out the trees, so compacted the thin layer of topsoil that even weeds could not sprout. Ludwig was forced to abandon his sophisticated machinery and revert to the traditional, labor-intensive, slash-and-burn method of clearing the jungle. Thousands of workers wielding machetes and chain saws completed the job, eventually clearing the trees from some 250,000 acres.

LEFT: Flames devour unusable logs and undergrowth as native trees are cleared away to permit planting of a domesticated forest.
ABOVE: Trees harvested for use at Jari head for the sawmill on the project's railroad.

A Wonder Tree Found Wanting

Ludwig based the enormous gamble of his Jari forestry project on the promise of a single tree, the gmelina. A native of Asia, this fast-growing tree reaches harvestable size on its home soil in six to 10 years, about one third the time required by comparable American trees.

Seedlings, carefully selected in Jari's horticulture nursery to correct the gmelina's genetic tendency to twist its trunk as it grows, were planted by the millions. Conventional forestry practices, including test plantings and crop diversification, were ignored. As a result, foresters overlooked the crucial fact that neither of Jari's two main types of soil—one sandy, one mostly clay—were hospitable to the gmelina. Tree growth was disastrously slow in the sandy soil, and only a bit better in the clay. Jari's production goals—1,500 tons of pulpwood and thousands of board feet of sawtimber daily—could not be met. Pulp production in 1981 was less than half the expected volume, sawtimber yields were inconsequential and Jari was deeply in debt. In fact, the native trees that had been spared during the initial land clearing had to be harvested to augment pulp production.

Workers hack away at the burgeoning jungle growth that constantly threatens to rob valuable nutrients from the thin soil of a young gmelina forest. Many Jari employees have to work full time battling the underbrush.

A hook lift hoists trimmed gmelina logs onto a truck. The logs went to the pulp mill for processing; branches and other debris were used as fuel for the Jari power plant.

A Last Resort

Convinced of the need to diversify the failing tree farm, a Jari employee defied Ludwig's orders in the late 1960s by secretly test-planting a stand of Caribbean pine next to the failing gmelina trees. A few years later, when Ludwig was shown the successful results of the planting, he ordered about a quarter of the gmelina plantations in the sandy soil to be replaced by the fast-growing pine. Another species, the tropical eucalyptus, was planted in 1979.

But the promise of the new plantations came too late for Ludwig's grandiose project. He had spent an average of $180,000 a day for 14 years to sustain it, and even his tremendous financial resources had been strained to the limit. In 1981 he sold the Jari Forest and Agricultural Company to a consortium of Brazilian interests. The new owners were determined to profit from Ludwig's mistakes and try again to harness the rainforest ecosystem, but many years—perhaps decades—are likely to pass before the outcome is clear.

Undaunted by the downpour that soaks the tropical forests daily, a Jari worker sets out seedlings of Caribbean pine in the ash of recently cleared and burned native forest.

Native jungle meets domesticated pine forest
on the Jari plantation. The pines were planted to
augment the initial gmelina stands but did
not mature in time to save Ludwig's project.

Chapter 6

RENEWING A LIVING RESOURCE

The rise of agriculture about 10,000 years ago augured ill for the world's forests. Although the first farming cultures arose on mostly treeless flood plains, such as the one between the Tigris and Euphrates Rivers in Mesopotamia, many forest dwellers soon became sowers and reapers. They relied on a method now known as slash-and-burn agriculture: They cut down a tract of forest, set fire to the undergrowth, planted and harvested the plot for a few years, and then, when the soil nutrients were depleted, abandoned it. Often the trees grew back after the humans departed, but sometimes poor soil, overgrazing by domesticated animals or some other factor prevented forest regeneration.

As civilizations expanded, more land was needed for agriculture, and more wood for construction and fuel. Geological and literary evidence suggests that Greece was covered by forests for thousands of years after the last ice age ended, around 8000 B.C. But by the Fourth Century B.C. the stark landscape left by deforestation and the ensuing severe erosion moved the philosopher Plato to compare the land of his native state of Attica to the "bones of a wasted body, the richer and softer parts of the soil having fallen away, and the mere skeleton of the land being left." Grazing by goats and sheep has prevented the regeneration of the natural forest; the olive and eucalyptus trees that are now common in Greece are descended from trees imported from Asia and Australia.

Some early cultures flourished in the forests. The Celts, for whom trees were objects of religious worship, established settlements in the primeval temperate forests of northwestern Europe. By medieval times, however, the decline of the European forests had accelerated as populations expanded and more land was cleared for agriculture. Firewood was always in demand, and with the emergence of metallurgy and other technologies requiring ever hotter flames, increasing numbers of trees were felled for processing into charcoal. By the year 1300, there were only 37 million acres of forest remaining in France, two million acres less than exist today. In some places, lumber was so scarce that a wooden coffin had to be rented for a funeral and then returned after the service to be used again.

The forests of Europe suffered further losses in the 16th Century as maritime warfare intensified and the demand for shipbuilding timbers grew. Oak, which was preferred over all other woods for building hulls, first became scarce in the countries surrounding the Mediterranean. When Philip II of Spain laid plans for his great Armada, his kingdom's oak forests were no longer extensive enough to supply all the required planks and

Arrow-straight, 300-foot-tall pines tower over recently planted seedlings in a carefully managed forest in Germany. Techniques such as genetic manipulation have increased the productivity of some species of trees by as much as 300 per cent.

beams, and he was forced to turn to northern countries whose woodlands had not yet been so heavily exploited. By the late 17th Century, England was importing from its colonies most of the long timbers required for ships' masts and keels. In North America, agents of the Crown carved a broad arrow—a mark of royal claim—into the trunks of the greatest and straightest of New England's white pines; these stately trees, some of them 300 feet tall, were perfect for the Royal Navy's masts.

As Americans spread westward across their heavily forested continent, they systematically cut down the trees for timber and to clear the land for agriculture. By the end of the 19th Century, some 400 years after the first Europeans arrived in the New World, very little of North America's original woodland remained. Already, a secondary forest had sprung up on lands that had been cleared and later abandoned. Some of this growth has since been harvested and has been replaced by a tertiary forest.

By comparison with its predecessors, this third growth is highly artificial. It lacks the rich diversity and random quality of the earlier woodlands and is in many respects more like a farm than a forest. This is because almost every forest is in some respects managed for enhanced productivity of wood, with results that are usually equivocal at best. There are, in the words of one biologist, "shortcomings, limitations and ecological complica-

In a seeming paradox, water is sprayed on delicate Douglas fir seedlings in a tree nursery in Washington State to protect them from an early fall frost. As the water turns to ice, it releases heat that keeps the seedlings from freezing.

tions" to treating natural resources as if they were business ventures.

But the agricultural approach to forestry is understandable, given the large and growing demand not only for wood but also for something called "multiple use." This phrase describes the expectation that forests should provide profits from timber, fuel and pulp, safe habitats for wildlife and recreation areas for people. But managing a forest for multiple use is exceedingly difficult, since it is by nature a constantly interacting community of countless living organisms, some of which will be considered beneficial to a particular use, some neutral and some harmful. Clearly, if the insistent human demands for multiple use are to be met, much of the wild forest—however esthetically appealing its complex ecosystem can be in the midst of civilization—must yield to engineered simplicity.

Indeed, much of the tertiary forest in both North America and Europe is the product of silviculture—the process of developing and raising varieties of trees selected for their ability to meet various human needs. The large-scale practice of silviculture began in Germany, and by the beginning of the 19th Century a forest of fast-growing, versatile conifers had been planted to keep the country well supplied and free from reliance on imported timber. Silviculture spread from there to other European countries and, eventually, to the United States.

Tree farmers strive to produce the maximum amount of commercially useful timber in the shortest time possible. They prepare the soil, plant, fertilize and harvest, as more conventional farmers do, and they are as likely to practice monoculture—the raising of just one type of plant—as is the farmer who devotes his fields entirely to soybeans or corn. For tree farmers, however, the wait for the harvest is a long one; their crop may not be ready for 30 or even 50 years.

To ensure that quality is as high as possible, silviculturists rely heavily on plant breeding. Foresters often search through stands of wild trees to find a superior variety and take cuttings. If the branches are too high to cut without scaling the tree, they are sometimes shot down with an ordinary rifle. These cuttings are taken to a nursery orchard, grafted onto vigorous saplings and nurtured until they produce seeds. The seeds, which carry the genes and hence the superior traits of the wild parent tree, are harvested and planted in yet another orchard to produce enough seedlings to be transplanted to commercial forests. Plant breeders also cross-pollinate nursery-raised seedlings to produce offspring that combine desirable traits of both parents.

Silviculturists have achieved enough precision to develop particular strains of trees for special purposes. A tree farm whose crop is to be used in the manufacture of high-quality paper, for example, can be provided with seedlings of specially bred trees whose tracheids—the water-conducting cells in the wood—have unusually thin walls. Conversely, trees with thick-walled tracheids have been developed to make pulp for coarser products such as cardboard or sturdy paper bags. The North Carolina State University Cooperative sponsors no fewer than 85 seed orchards, each one seeking trees with a different combination of characteristics. The work is closely coordinated, and a plant that is unsatisfactory for newsprint manufacturing, for instance, can be handed over to another nursery that is testing seedlings for lumber production or tissue paper.

One trait always desired in trees meant for use in monoculture is resis-

Forest Cultures for the Future

In the commercial forest of the future, every tree may be a clone—an exact genetic copy of a desirable parent tree from which tissue was removed for culturing in a laboratory. A forest of such trees could be twice as productive as its most carefully bred and managed counterpart of the late 20th Century.

Tissue-culture techniques are still in the experimental stages, but foresters schooled in genetics have successfully crossbred and propagated superior strains of trees. Drawing on the great diversity of traits found in both wild and cultivated trees, foresters graft cuttings of select trees onto nursery stock. Bags slipped over a grafted plant's female flowers prevent random pollination by the wind, and pollen taken from a second plant selected for crossbreeding is injected into the bag. If the offspring of the cross show a desirable mix of traits, they are planted in an orchard where they produce seed that is gathered for large-scale commercial planting.

Offspring can be obtained from a superior tree with still another technique, called air layering. The tips of the branches are treated with a hormone that prompts roots to form; when severed and planted, each plantling will grow into an exact replica of its single parent.

GRAFTING A CUTTING

POLLINATING BY HAND

APPLYING ROOTING HORMONE

CULTURING FIR TISSUE

tance to pests and diseases; an infection or infestation that would be slowed by the varying characteristics of a mixed forest can devastate a tract containing only one variety of tree. In some plantations in the Southeast, 60 per cent of the pines are infected with the often lethal fusiform rust fungus, which destroys about 20 million dollars' worth of trees every year. Foresters are optimistic, however, that the rate of infection will decline sharply in the near future as vulnerable varieties are replaced by specially selected rust-resistant varieties.

While they expect to have to deal with various pests, foresters are sometimes dismayed to find that their management practices have elicited a surprisingly strong backlash from the wildlife that is normally thought of as a benign part of the forest ecosystem. Such has been the case in parts of England and Scotland, where conifers were planted on hundreds of thousands of acres after World War I. These areas had once supported hardwood forests, but the trees had been cut generations before to accommodate the needs of a growing population. During the War, Germany's U-boats had disrupted shipping and greatly restricted Great Britain's timber imports, and the nation resolved to regenerate its domestic woodlands so it could be self-sufficient in any future conflict.

Sitka spruce, imported from North America, grew so well on the deforested land that it soon became the overwhelmingly dominant species in the extensive managed forests. As decades passed, the forest managers became concerned about a number of problems associated with monoculture, including a lack of diversity in not only the trees but the birds, insects and other animals living in the monotonous tracts.

When the time came to replant the forest, British government foresters decided to include various hardwoods in the plantings, both for the value of the wood and for the diversity they would lend the environment. Oak, beech, birch and ash were planted among the conifers, and the managers were promptly confronted by a serious, and seemingly insoluble, problem: It weighed about 50 pounds, possessed admirable grace and strength, and had dark, limpid eyes. It is called the roe deer.

Roe deer relish the spring shoots of hardwoods such as those planted among the Sitka spruces. And like all deer, the roe are equipped for the survival of their species with a remarkable fecundity that is normally held in check by the starvation of those animals that cannot find food. When the foresters unwittingly provided an abundant food supply, the deer population promptly exploded. Soon the animals were devouring young trees almost as fast as they could be planted—Sitka spruce as well as hardwoods.

The only solution was to replace the control on the deer population that had once been exerted by starvation. Thus, for forest after forest, government managers proposed raising the quotas for roe deer that they and local hunters could shoot. But the animals are so elusive that deer counters were hard pressed to come up with true population figures. Careful head counts in small sections of Britain showed that local estimates, even those of veteran foresters, were on the average only one third of reality, which meant that the cull rates set by the authorities were far too low to be effective. Under

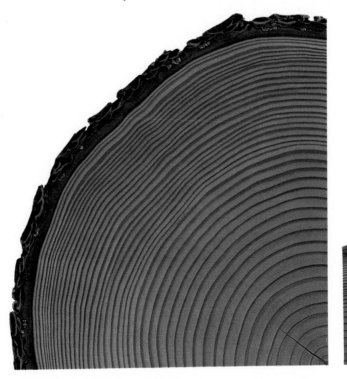

Cross sections of two 40-year-old Douglas firs show the effects of forest management. The larger tree grew in a stand that was regularly thinned, while intense competition for sunlight, nutrients and water in an overcrowded plot slowed the growth of the other.

153

A patchwork of managed forest plots—dark Monterey pines, rich green Douglas firs and larches that are bare and brown because it is winter—quilt the

mountainous countryside of Golden Downs, New Zealand. Eventually, each tract will be clear-cut for paper pulp and lumber.

The logger clear-cutting the spruce forest at left can fell about 12 trees an hour with a chain saw. In the same period, a person using a feller-layer (*above*) can shear off five times as many trees and lay them neatly aside for collection.

these circumstances, most hardwoods never came close to maturity, and foresters had to continue to rely heavily on Sitka spruce, which seemed to be a less-preferred item in the deer diet.

Usually it is not the wildlife that interferes with forest management but the other way around, perhaps most dramatically when loggers make use of the controversial practice known as clear-cutting. Often associated with monoculture, clear-cutting involves the wholesale cutting of large tracts of trees at once, leaving a temporarily savaged landscape. Environmentalists complain that clear-cutting is damaging to wildlife, but when a research organization studied the relationship in 1979, its report was ambivalent.

The Intensive Management Practices Assessment Center—a cooperative venture of the U.S. Forest Service, the University of Florida and the logging industry—studied commercial pine forests in Florida. It found that when a forest is clear-cut, birds and mammals that fed or nested in the canopy must immediately migrate to a new area; on the other hand, species such as deer, rabbits, quail and turkeys prosper when the trees are gone, because the increased levels of sunshine promote rapid new growth of the grasses and other ground-hugging plants on which they feed. According to the center's report, "To argue that one community is better or worse than the other is academic."

The key to the nature of the impact of clear-cutting on wildlife, the researchers found, is not the size of the area clear-cut but the relationship of its size and shape. A circular 100-acre clearing, they found, can have a greater negative effect on wildlife than a cleared area that is

156

five times as big but is narrow and sinuous in shape and follows the natural contours of the land. The wild animals that benefit from the sudden growth of ground plants after removal of the forest like to stay close to cover while feeding; they would seldom venture into the center of a large area, but they would be able to make use of all of the new growth in a narrow strip. And if the clear-cut area conforms with the land's contours, subsequent erosion of soil and nutrients will be much less than is the case when steep slopes are cleared.

Clear-cutting creates problems that go beyond the welfare of wild animals, and the worst of these is erosion. Robbed of its protective cover and torn by the movement of heavy machinery, the exposed land immediately begins to wash away. If the slope is steep, or if new seedlings or some other cover crop is not planted promptly, the damage can be severe. A study of a clear-cut site in New Hampshire showed that accelerated runoff from the stripped area greatly increased the flow of nearby streams and multiplied by several times their content of silt and dissolved chemicals—calcium, potassium and other essential plant nutrients. Thus, what soil was left in place was impoverished. However, soil moisture content and temperature were both raised, with the effect of encouraging new growth.

Such studies have led to a number of recommendations for limiting the negative effects of clear-cutting. Researchers recommend that it be done over relatively small areas on gentle slopes where soil fertility is high. And they suggest that commercially unimportant forest plants such as elderberry, raspberry and pin cherry be allowed to grow back, since they play an important role in the forest's recovery process by quickly storing nutrients and reducing erosion.

Properly managed clear-cutting appears to have a necessary place in the lumber industry. One large United States timber company maintains that on some large tracts, clear-cutting is both economically and biologically efficient. In the words of a company official, "While people generally accept that one should grow trees in order to harvest them, it's less often realized that the reverse is also true; to grow new trees, you first have to cut the old ones. But with 30- to 50-year growing cycles, tomorrow's commercially useful softwoods have to be in the ground and stretching for sunlight today—and clear-cutting is a tool for getting them there quickly, in massive quantities, with the best chance for survival and growth."

As a new forest grows on a clear-cut site, the losses in nutrients are made up, and the ecosystem returns to its previous balance. But the process takes time. Scientists have found that in Northern hardwood forests, the period required is 60 to 80 years, and the U.S. Forest Service recommends that, to be on the safe side, some clear-cut sites not be harvested again for as long as 110 to 120 years. If the new forest is cut before its natural balance has been regained, the result could be long-term degradation of the ecosystem, making it less and less suitable for growing trees.

One manifestation of the tendency of demand for wood to outstrip supply is the fact that in the United States, except for government-owned wilderness areas in the West that are off-limits to the logging industry, the truly tall trees are gone. The great white pines of the Northeast are coming back, but they have not achieved the majestic size of the native trees they replaced. The story is the same in the Great Lakes region and in the hardwood forests that spread east and west from the Appalachian Mountains. In the

South, where cultivated loblolly pines are harvested every 25 to 30 years, loggers are felling smaller trees than they did in years past. The economic consequences are significant because the productivity of a tree declines with the square of its diameter; a 30-inch log yields only a quarter as much marketable lumber as a 60-inch log of the same length.

The need to cut more individual trees to get the same volume of lumber has, of course, dictated a change in technology. The giant chain saws that were once needed to bring down enormous trees have been replaced in many situations with hydraulically powered shears, mounted on tractors, that cut the smaller trees off at the base. In past times, loggers would cut the tops off the trees and harvest only the lower, limbless portions of the trunks. Now, in order to get longer and more valuable logs from smaller trees, the tops are retained and machines strip the trunks of all their limbs. One such device consists of a telescoping boom equipped with knives that remove the limbs before the trees are felled.

In many forests only selected trees are cut. The more mature trees may be harvested from a stand of younger or less valuable trees, or the younger trees may be felled, leaving the larger trees to shelter new growth. Such methods present the problem of gathering scattered logs into bunches large enough to be hauled out of the forest efficiently. One solution is an ungainly two-wheeled machine called the Menzi Muck. It is equipped with a hydraulic boom that steadies it as it makes its way up steep slopes (looking like a "large, wounded spider," says one observer), and a powerful arm that shears off the trees and piles them up for later removal by huge tractors. These new machines are impressive but also expensive, and their use has only maintained the productivity achieved during the days of old-growth logging when larger trees were available for harvest.

A further problem posed by the small-tree forest is that its wood is less desirable for use as lumber than that from large trees, and the demand for high-grade lumber continues unabated. A mitigating factor is that the need for lower-grade wood is also rising. The demand for pulpwood for paper manufacture, for instance, has expanded dramatically during the last half century. There is also a great and growing demand for reconstituted wood products such as chipboard and plywood, which can be manufactured with low-quality wood.

The commercial demands on the forest will surely increase in the future, and there is no certainty that any combination of applied technology, silviculture and forest management will be able to boost productivity at the same rate. One way out of the dilemma may be to find sources other than trees for the woody tissue that is required in the manufacturing of certain products.

Among the most promising alternatives to wood in paper production is kenaf, a fast-growing annual herb that is native to Africa. The fibers of its 15-foot-tall stems have long been used for making rope, and the U.S. Department of Agriculture, which began experimenting with kenaf as a source of pulp for paper in the 1950s, has found it the equal of wood. Kenaf makes a bright, strong newsprint that does not turn yellow because it does not contain lignin, which causes wood-based paper to discolor when it is exposed to light. The harvested plant is easy to store and grind up for milling, and processing it into paper requires less chemical treatment and less energy. Furthermore, while pine trees take 30 years to grow large enough to

Log booms on British Columbia's Georgia Strait, each one held together by logs chained end to end around the perimeter, permit tugboats to tow as much as 12,000 cords of wood at a time to a paper-pulp mill.

harvest for wood pulp, kenaf grows from seed to maturity in just 150 days. A field of kenaf produces three to five times as much dry material each year as an equal area planted with pulpwood trees.

In 1982, the American Newspaper Publishers Association, having seen the cost of newsprint more than double in a decade, joined with several other interested groups to form an organization called Kenaf International. After making a thorough study of the economics of papermaking, Kenaf International estimated that a ton of kenaf newsprint might cost only a tenth as much as the standard variety, or even less. Yet it is hard to teach old dogs new tricks. The climate in the American South is ideally suited to growing kenaf, but few farmers there have chosen to grow it in place of traditional crops, perhaps because the long-term economic benefit of kenaf farming has yet to be proved conclusively. Paper manufacturers have been as reluctant as farmers to opt for change. But as demand for paper climbs, it is likely that the raw materials for newsprint will, in fact, be grown on conventional farms, leaving tree farms to supply timber for other purposes. And kenaf is not the only possible newsprint crop. Wheat straw, sugar-cane fibers and several grasses have all shown promise.

Economics are much different outside the industrialized nations. All through the developing world, wood is used primarily as a fuel. Rising needs have led to a tremendous annual loss of forest cover, followed by losses of topsoil and increases in water runoff. Kenya, which is relatively well off among the less developed countries, derives three quarters of its energy consumption from wood, and Kenyans are consuming their nation's firewood supply six times faster than it is being replenished, a trend that can lead only to disaster. The trend is accelerated by the general practice of gathering firewood in the form of easily cut and readily carried saplings,

Silt that washed from this slope in New Zealand after the forest was clear-cut and burned in the late 19th Century has completely clogged the bed of the river at its base. Although trees have been reestablished nearby, unstable soil and the steepness of the grade have defeated every attempt to reforest the slope.

Prompt planting of Douglas fir seedlings helped a mountaintop site in Oregon resist erosion after it was clear-cut. Red-tinted maples, alders and other plants that have sprung up naturally also help hold the soil.

with the result that mature trees dominate Kenya's forests and few young ones are coming along for the future.

No satisfactory plan for dealing with Kenya's impending wood crisis has emerged. Planting fast-growing trees on unforested land—a technique called afforestation—holds some promise, but the best time for planting trees in Kenya is also the best time for planting food crops. Most Kenyans are working on farms and do not have time to set out tree seedlings. Another proposal, aimed at finding an alternative source of energy, is to create plantations for growing crops such as corn and potatoes and use them to produce ethanol, a form of alcohol that can be used in combination with petroleum fuels. But such an ambitious program takes money, and in Kenya, which spends a third of its foreign exchange on costly imported oil, money is in short supply. Still another possibility is to design modestly priced stoves that make highly efficient use of wood fuel. But for the time being, Kenya is locked in the same cycle of decline that ensnares most of the world's population and many of the world's forests.

In the Indian state of Madhya Pradesh, for example, about a third of the land is forested. Madhya Pradesh has long exported lumber and firewood to other parts of India, but the government has failed in its attempts to plant trees to replace the ones harvested or to create woodland commons to meet the requirements of villages. Many inhabitants are so pressed by daily needs that they cannot see the advantage of long-range government plans. They regularly collect firewood and allow their livestock to browse in the forest reserves in defiance of state law, destroying seedlings and weakening older plants. If the loss of forests continues unabated, much of the state will be stripped of trees by the end of this century.

But India, which struggles under the multiple burdens of overpopulation, poverty and widespread public indifference to the loss of natural resources, also has within its borders an example of what can be achieved by forestry programs.

Gujarat, next door to Madhya Pradesh, is one of the most tree-poor states in India. Two decades ago a small and shrinking fraction of the wood consumed in the state was from local sources; the rest was imported at a high cost. But in 1973, the government of Gujarat embarked on a program to encourage its residents to plant wood lots to reduce the drain on the state's few forests. Local village councils and the state would share in the proceeds of harvesting local forests. Individual citizens would enjoy cheaper and more plentiful wood and were to be responsible for the health of the wooded tracts.

Five years after the start of the program, one sixth of the state's villages had established new woodland plots, and more villages were following suit each year. Protected from foraging livestock, the woodlands developed harvestable grass, fruit trees and, eventually, timber. Careful tree selection has made some wood lots unusually productive in a short time. One eucalyptus hybrid, for instance, grows at the astonishing rate of 15 feet or more a year. When the tree is cut down, at about five years of age, the stump quickly sends up new stems. Hardly a scrap of the harvest goes to waste. Leaves, bark and branches serve as fuel, while the trunk provides lumber.

There are now unfenced wood lots in and around many Gujarat villages and they are free of the depredations usually associated with such woodlands in poor nations. The state remains an importer of fuel wood, but the government's initiative will make it far more self-sufficient. Part of this very positive trend can be attributed to a relatively high literacy rate, part to a good and efficiently administered plan, and part to the spirit of cooperation that characterizes the people of Gujarat. Whatever the causes, the success in Gujarat and the dismal failure in neighboring Madhya Pradesh suggest the array of complexities that must be dealt with in seeking to relieve a desperate situation in an overpopulated and resource-poor land.

India is not the only such country where carefully selected tree varieties are proving their importance. In the Philippines and Mexico, foresters are experimenting with the Leucaena, a genus that flourishes in many tropical areas. One variety, dubbed the Hawaiian Giant, grows 10 feet a year and reaches an ultimate height of 60 feet. Hawaiian Giants destined to be harvested at a smaller size can be planted as densely as a corn field, for the trees have long taproots that do not interfere with those of their neighbors. The deep roots allow the Leucaena to draw on water sources far below the surface and thus withstand drought.

A member of the legume family, the Leucaena adapts well to poor soil, thanks to the rhizobium bacteria that colonize its roots and form nodules that capture nitrogen from the air. By combining the nitrogen with hydrogen, the bacteria produce compounds that the host tree uses to synthesize proteins and build new tissue. Much of the nitrogen fixed by the bacteria accumulates in the Leucaena's leaves, which can be harvested and spread around food crops as fertilizer—a boon for farmers too poor to afford commercial fertilizers.

Yet such glimmers of hope are rare in Asia, Africa and South America, where 90 per cent of the world's people live. In Nepal, firewood costs more than kerosene. The shortage of firewood is so great in India that 400 million

In the cool, mountainous countryside of Nepal (*above*) every individual needs almost a cord of firewood a year for heating and cooking. Fifty per cent of Nepal's upland forests have been felled for fuel since 1950, leaving entire mountainsides denuded (*right*).

tons of cow dung are burned annually, depriving the fields of a valuable source of fertilizer. Throughout the underdeveloped world, crop residues are being burned as fuel instead of being allowed to decay and enrich the soil. Overall, the planet's forests are in retreat, and without vigorous attempts to reverse this process, the level of human suffering on the globe will surely increase in the decades to come. For all of our expertise in fashioning things of metal and plastics, and in locating and mining fossil fuels, we remain fundamentally dependent on wood.

Industrialized nations not only see the crisis that lies ahead but can afford the remedy of extensive forestation. According to a U.S. State Department study conducted in the late 1970s, the industrialized nations are three times richer in forest resources per capita than the underdeveloped nations. The report estimates that by the end of the century the extent of forests in the Northern Hemisphere, where most industrialized nations are located, will be unchanged, while the smaller forests of the Southern Hemisphere will

China's Versatile Paulownia Tree

In 1958, Chairman Mao Tse-tung of the People's Republic of China proposed that every rural family plant a tree at each corner of their dwelling. Mao's exhortation was the opening note in a long campaign to meet the country's pressing need for wood, an effort that soon had people planting trees in every conceivable place—along roads, rivers, canals and even the boundaries between fields. The tree most favored for these plantings was a native called the paulownia.

With their astonishing growth rate of as much as eight feet per year, paulownias were ready for harvest in less than a decade. And their increasing pervasiveness yielded many dividends: medicinal ingredients from the bark and flowers, animal fodder and soil nutrients from the leaves, and protection from wind erosion. Plantings of the amazing tree tripled in China between 1970 and 1980 and soon made a major contribution to an adequate wood supply for the country's more than one billion people.

Six-month-old paulownia saplings spread umbrella-like leaves over a nursery worker in Hubei province *(left)*. At bottom, a silviculturist measures an eight-year-old tree whose circumference is six feet.

have shrunk by 40 per cent. And the high rate of population growth in the latter group will make the disparity in per capita forest wealth far greater. Much of the world's population will thus be deprived of wood for burning and building, and of the prospects for development offered by possession of the many raw materials to be found in the forest.

Cellulose, a major component of trees, is critical to the manufacture of many plastics and may become even more important as petroleum grows scarcer and more expensive. It is also used in glues, film, textiles and explosives. Charcoal, made by burning wood in a kiln that limits the oxygen supply, is in demand not only for cooking but also for various industrial and agricultural processes, for filtering and purifying air, water and sewage, and as a pigment for ink. Resins are used by papermakers to coat their product and prevent inks from smudging. They are also essential in the production of varnishes, rubber, soap, detergents and adhesives. Turpentine remains important not only as a solvent but also as a source of chemicals used in making perfume, disinfectants and artificial flavors.

The bark of a species of oak grown mostly in the Mediterranean countries of Europe and Africa supplies the world with all of its cork. Bamboo, which has been cultivated for thousands of years, has canes strong enough to serve as reinforcing rods in concrete walls, and pulp that can be processed into paper. Bamboo shoots can be added to the human diet, and young leaves make nutritious animal fodder. India and Sri Lanka export tons of a fiber

Italian workers construct a traditional earth kiln for converting wood to charcoal. After being covered with a layer of turf, the wood is lighted and allowed to smolder for 10 days. The fire is then smothered and the charcoal removed for use in household cooking and heating.

called coir, derived from the husks of coconuts and used for mattress stuffing and brush bristles. Indonesian forest palms yield thousands of tons of rattan for furniture. Each year, Thailand exports 17,000 tons of kapok, a floss produced in the seed pods of the gigantic kapok tree and used as insulation and as a stuffing material for life jackets.

The list of foodstuffs produced by forest plants ranges from such fruits as bananas, papayas, dates and mangoes to vanilla, coffee, cocoa and a host of nuts and spices. With a finite amount of agricultural land available in the world, and with populations growing, forests will have to be managed to increase their output of food. In Great Britain, for example, researchers are experimentally pulping and processing protein-rich tree leaves into a product as nutritionally valuable as meat.

And, of course, forests are vast stores of energy. The commercial forests of the United States alone contain enough energy to supply the entire world's needs for a year. Through selection of better stock and by more intensive forest management, the yield per acre of loblolly pine in the southeastern United States has tripled since 1960 and is expected to increase still further. In the United States, cellulose-derived ethanol could provide 10 per cent of all the energy required by the year 2000. In Brazil, where for several years all new automobiles have been designed to run on an ethanol mixture, chemists have discovered that a certain native tree, the copaifera, produces an oil so similar to diesel oil that it seems a nearly perfect fuel for internal combustion engines. Since fuels from trees and other vegetable materials are relatively free of sulfur, their use would help eliminate the damaging acid rain that forms as a result of fossil-fuel combustion.

Many nations, having realized the value and promise of their forest resources, have confronted the tasks of maintenance and renewal with innovative and rigorous management. The problems are enormous and complex, and whether the forests of the future can fulfill all of the demands of humanity remains in doubt. But with continued success in plant breeding, crop selection and forestry practices, there is reason to hope that the growing of trees may soon be profitable enough to become even more extensive—on salty wastelands, on dry savannas and on the very lands from which the forest was once driven to make room for agriculture. Ω

A plantation of hybrid white poplars developed by Italian silviculturists flourishes on a low-lying, sandy plain despite twice-yearly flooding from the

nearby Po and Oglio Rivers. The fast-growing and disease-resistant poplars are felled at about 10 years of age to supply pulp to the paper industry.

ACKNOWLEDGMENTS

For their help in the preparation of this book the editors wish to thank: In Canada: Edmonton—Dr. Ruth Stockey, Department of Botany, University of Alberta; Ottawa—F.L.C. Reed, Assistant Deputy Minister, Canadian Forest Service. *In Finland:* Helsinki—Simo Hannelius, Metsäkuva-Arkisto Ky. *In France:* Fontainebleau—Jean-Pierre Chasseau, Office National des Forêts; Nancy—Joanny Guillard, Marie-Jeanne Lionnet, École Nationale du Génie Rural des Eaux et des Forêts; Paris—Jean Gachet, Office National des Forêts. *In Great Britain:* Oxford—H. C. Dawkins. *In Italy:* Bologna—Laura Miani Belletti, Biblioteca Universitaria; Florence—Raffaello Giannini, Piero Piussi, Istituto di Selvicoltura, Università di Firenze; Rome—Lucio Bortolotti, Ministero Agricoltura e Foreste; Florita Botts, Giuditta Dolci-Favi, Ted Pasca, Food and Agriculture Organization of the United Nations. *In the Netherlands:* Rotterdam—J.R.P. Van Hoey Smith. *In the People's Republic of China:* Beijing—The Bureau of Agriculture and Forestry; Zaho Fang, New China Pictures Co. *In the United States:* District of Columbia—Laurence D. Wiseman, Vice President, Planning & Development, American Forest Institute; Dr. Robert A. DeFilipps, Office of Biological Conservation, Smithsonian Institution; Dr. Stanley L. Krugman, Carl Puuri, Timber Management Research, Michael J. Rogers, Fire Prevention and Fuels Management, United States Department of Agriculture (USDA) Forest Service; Robert Goodland, Office of Environmental Affairs, The World Bank; Dr. Thomas Lovejoy, Peter Oyens, World Wildlife Fund; Florida—(Gainesville) Dr. Nigel J. H. Smith, Department of Geography, Dr. Charles Wagley, Graduate Research Professor of Anthropology, Center for Latin American Studies, University of Florida; Colorado—(Denver) Dr. Jack A. Wolfe, Paleontology and Stratigraphy Branch, U.S. Geographical Survey; Georgia—(Dry Branch) C. Wayne Adkins, Scientific and Technical Photographer, Charles K. McMahon, Project Leader, Southern Forest Fire Laboratory, USDA Forest Service; Maryland—(Baltimore) Dr. Grace S. Brush, Department of Geography and Environmental Engineering, The Johns Hopkins University; (Beltsville) Dr. Miklos Faust, Fruit Laboratory, USDA Agricultural Research Center; (Cabin John) Trudy Nicholson; Massachusetts—(Petersham) Professor Ernest Gould, Harvard Forest; Montana—(Missoula) Aerial Fire Depot; Hal E. Anderson, Research Supervisory Physicist, Charles George, Donald Latham, Northern Forest Fire Laboratory, USDA Forest Service; Edward Heilman, Director, Aviation and Fire Management, Northern Region, USDA Forest Service; New York—(New York) Dr. Bruce W. McAlpin, Department of Biology, Hunter College; (Syracuse) Dr. Wilfred A. Côté, Director, Center for Ultrastructure Studies, State University of New York; (Woodstock) Richard Crist; North Carolina—(Durham) Professor William Davis, School of Forestry and Environmental Studies, Duke University; Oregon—(Portland) Mike Ferris, Pacific Northwest Region, USDA Forest Service; Pennsylvania—(Maytown) Lloyd K. Townsend; Virginia—(Burke) Bill Hezlep; Washington—(Takoma) Michael Wotton, Manager of Technical Communication, Weyerhaeuser Company. *In West Germany:* Bonn—Heinz-Hugo von Unruh; Göttingen—Horst Rienecke, Schutzgemeinschaft Deutscher Wald; Professor Bernhard Ulrich; Hamburg—Susanne Schapowalow; Neuenstein—G. P. Frohmaier, Silvatec, GMBH.

Particularly useful sources of information and quotations used in this volume were: *Biology of Plants* by Peter H. Raven, Ray F. Evert and Helena Curtis, Worth Publishers, 1976; *Evolution and Plants of the Past* by Harlan P. Banks, Wadsworth Publishing, 1970; *Fire and Ecosystems,* edited by T. T. Kozlowski, Academic Press, 1974; *Fire in America: A Cultural History of Wildland and Rural Fire* by Stephen J. Pyne, Princeton University Press, 1982; *Forest Fire Control and Use* by Arthur A. Brown and Kenneth P. Davis, McGraw-Hill, 1973; *The International Book of the Forest,* edited by Mitchell Beazley, Mitchell Beazley Publishers, 1981; *The International Book of Trees* by Hugh Johnson, Mitchell Beazley, 1980; *Jungles,* edited by Edward S. Ayensu, Crown, 1980; *Physiology of Woody Plants* by Paul J. Kramer and Theodore T. Kozlowski, Academic Press, 1979.

The index was prepared by Gisela S. Knight.

BIBLIOGRAPHY

Books

Adams, Kramer, *The Redwoods.* Popular Library (Warner-Random House), 1969.

Andrews, Henry N., Jr.:
Ancient Plants and the World They Lived In. Comstock Publishing, 1947.
Studies in Paleobotany. John Wiley & Sons, 1961.

Arnold, Chester A., *An Introduction to Paleobotany.* McGraw-Hill, 1947.

Ash, Sidney R., and David D. May, *Petrified Forest: The Story behind the Scenery.* Petrified Forest Museum Association, 1969.

Ayensu, Edward S., ed., *Jungles.* Crown, 1980.

Bailey, Liberty Hyde and Ethel Zoe, *Hortus Third: A Concise Dictionary of Plants Cultivated in the United States and Canada.* Macmillan, 1976.

Banks, Harlan P., *Evolution and Plants of the Past.* Wadsworth Publishing, 1970.

Beazley, Mitchell, ed., *The International Book of the Forest.* Mitchell Beazley, 1981.

Beddall, Barbara G., ed., *Wallace and Bates in the Tropics: An Introduction to the Theory of Natural Selection.* Macmillan, 1969.

Brown, Arthur A., and Kenneth P. Davis, *Forest Fire Control and Use.* McGraw-Hill, 1973.

Coats, Alice M., *The Plant Hunters.* McGraw-Hill, 1969.

Conway, Steve, *Logging Practices: Principles of Timber Harvesting Systems.* Miller Freeman Publications, 1982.

Daubenmire, Rexford:
Plant Communities: A Textbook of Plant Synecology. Harper & Row, 1968.
Plant Geography. Academic Press, 1978.

Emsley, Michael, *Rain Forests and Cloud Forests.* Harry N. Abrams, 1979.

Everett, Thomas H., *Living Trees of the World.* Doubleday, 1969.

Farb, Peter, and the Editors of Time-Life Books, *The Forest.* Time-Life Books, 1980.

Fernow, Bernhard E., *A Brief History of Forestry.* Toronto: University Press, 1911.

Flint, Richard Foster, *The Earth and Its History.* W. W. Norton & Company, 1973.

Foster, Adriance S., and Ernest M. Gifford Jr., *Comparative Morphology of Vascular Plants.* W. H. Freeman, 1974.

Francis, Wilfrid, *Coal: Its Formation and Composition.* London: Edward Arnold, 1961.

Fuller, Harry J., and Oswald Tippo, *College Botany.* Henry Holt, 1954.

Guide to Trees. Simon and Schuster, 1978.

Harlow, William M., *Inside Wood: Masterpiece of Nature.* American Forestry Association, 1970.

Holmes, Sandra, *Trees of the World.* Grosset & Dunlap, 1975.

Hora, Bayard, ed., *The Oxford Encyclopedia of Trees of the World.* Oxford University Press, 1981.

Janssen, Raymond E., *Leaves and Stems from Fossil Forests: A Handbook of the Paleobotanical Collections in the Illinois State Museum.* Illinois State Museum, 1979.

Johnson, Hugh, *The International Book of Trees.* Mitchell Beazley, 1980.

Johnson, Warren T., and Howard H. Lyon, *Insects That Feed on Trees and Shrubs.* Cornell University Press, 1976.

Ketchum, Richard M., *The Secret Life of the Forest.* American Heritage Press, 1970.

Kozlowski, Theodore T., ed., *Fire and Ecosystems.* Academic Press, 1974.

Kramer, Paul J., and Theodore T. Kozlowski, *Physiology of Woody Plants.* Academic Press, 1979.

Leathart, Scott, *Trees of the World.* A & W Publishers, 1977.

Luke, R. H., and A. G. McArthur, *Bushfires in Australia.* Canberra: Australian Government Publishing Service, 1978.

McCormick, Jack, *The Life of the Forest.* McGraw-Hill, 1966.

McGeary, M. Nelson, *Gifford Pinchot: Forester, Politician.* Princeton University Press, 1960.

Martin, J. T., and B. E. Juniper, *The Cuticles of Plants.* St. Martin's Press, 1970.

Menninger, Edwin A., *Fantastic Trees.* Viking Press, 1967.

Metcalf, C. L., and W. P. Flint, *Destructive and Useful Insects: Their Habits and Control.* McGraw-Hill, 1962.

Meyer, Bernard S., Donald B. Anderson, Richard H. Bohning and Douglas G. Fratianne, *Introduction to Plant Physiology.* Van Nostrand, 1973.

Moore, Tui De Roy, *Galapagos: Islands Lost in Time.* Viking Press, 1980.

Moran, Emilio F., *Developing the Amazon.* Indiana University Press, 1981.

Naden, Corinne J., *Woodlands around the World.* Franklin Watts, 1973.

The New America's Wonderlands: Our National Parks. National Geographic, 1980.

Ovington, J. D., *Woodlands.* London: The English Universities Press, 1965.

Pagel, Walter, *Joan Baptista Van Helmont.* Cambridge University Press, 1981.

Peattie, Donald Culross:
A Natural History of Trees of Eastern and Central North America. Houghton Mifflin, 1950.
A Natural History of Western Trees. Riverside Press, 1953.

Pinchot, Gifford, *Breaking New Ground.* Harcourt, Brace, 1947.

Pyne, Stephen J., *Fire in America: A Cultural History of Wildland and Rural Fire.* Princeton University Press, 1982.

Raven, Peter H., Ray F. Evert and Helena Curtis, *Biology of Plants.* Worth Publishers, 1976.

Reynolds, Vernon, *Budongo: An African Forest and Its Chimpanzees.* Natural History Press, 1965.

Richards, Paul W., *The Life of the Jungle.* McGraw-Hill, 1970.

Scenic Wonders of America. Reader's Digest, 1980.

Selsam, Millicent E., *Birth of a Forest.* Harper & Row, 1964.

Silverberg, Robert, *The World of the Rain Forest.* Meredith Press, 1967.

Smith, David Martyn, *The Practice of Silviculture.* John Wiley & Sons, 1962.

Smith, Nigel J. H., *Rainforest Corridors: The Transamazon Colonization Scheme.* University of California Press, 1982.

Spurr, Stephen H., and Burton V. Barnes, *Forest Ecology.* John Wiley & Sons, 1980.

Steen, Harold K., *The U.S. Forest Service: A History.* University of Washington Press, 1976.

Stratton, Joanna L., *Pioneer Women.* Simon and Schuster, 1982.

Turnbull, Colin M., *Wayward Servants: The Two Worlds of the African Pygmies.* Natural History Press, 1965.

Westcott, Cynthia:
The Gardener's Bug Book. Doubleday, 1973.
Plant Disease Handbook. Van Nostrand Reinhold, 1971.

Wilson, Carl L., and Walter E. Loomis, *Botany.* Holt, Rinehart and Winston, 1964.

Wright, Henry A., and Arthur W. Bailey, *Fire Ecology: United States and Southern Canada.* John Wiley & Sons, 1982.

Zwinger, Ann H., and Beatrice E. Willard, *Land above the Trees: A Guide to American Alpine Tundra.* Harper & Row, 1972.

Periodicals

Agarwal, Anil, "The Forgotten Energy Crisis." *New Scientist,* February 10, 1983.

Arnold, J.E.M., and Jules Jongma, "Fuelwood and Charcoal in Developing Countries." *Unasylva,* Vol. 29, No. 118.

Barrett, Stephen W., "Indians and Fire." *Western Wildlands,* Spring 1980.

Batten, Mary, "The Cradle of Life." *Science Digest,* July 1981.

"Billionaire Ludwig's Brazilian Gamble." *Time,* September 10, 1979.

Brown, Lester R., "Reforesting the Earth." *American Forests,* February 1982.

Brush, Grace S., "An Environmental Analysis of Forest Patterns." *American Scientist,* January/February 1982.

Calvin, Melvin, "New Sources for Fuel and Materials." *Science,* January 7, 1983.

Chelminski, Rudolph, "A Fungus Beats the Chestnut Blight at Its Own Game." *Smithsonian,* June 1979.

Cherfas, Jeremy, "Trees Have Made Man Upright." *New Scientist,* January 20, 1983.

Cock, James H., "Cassava: A Basic Energy Source in the Tropics." *Science,* November 19, 1982.

Cowling, Ellis B., and Charles B. Davey, "Acid Precipitation: Basic Principles and Ecological Consequences." *Pulp and Paper,* August 1981.

Deans, Nora Lynne, "An Underwater Jungle: Journey through a Mangrove Swamp." *Oceans,* July 1982.

Deevey, E. S., et al., "Mayan Urbanism: Impact on a Tropical Karst Environment." *Science,* October 19, 1979.

Delcourt, Hazel R., "The Virtue of Forests, Virgin and Otherwise." *Natural History,* June 1981.

Dubos, René, " 'Replenish the Earth, and Subdue It': Human Touch Often Improves the Land." *Smithsonian,* December 1972.

Eckholm, Erik, "Forest Renewal in India." *Natural History,* June/July 1979.

"Energy and Chemicals from Trees." *Science,* March 12, 1982.

Farnum, Peter, Roger Timmis and J. Laurence Kulp, "Biotechnology of Forest Yield." *Science,* February 11, 1983.

Fischer, William C., "Fire Management Techniques for the 1980's." *The 1980 Ames Forester,* Vol. 66.

Gall, Norman, "Ludwig's Amazon Empire." *Forbes,* May 14, 1979.

Goldring, Winifred, "The Upper Devonian Forest of Seed Ferns in Eastern New York." *New York State Museum Bulletin,* March 1974.

Gorham, Eville, "What to Do about Acid Rain." *Technology Review,* October 1982.

Gorney, Cynthia, "The Last Frontier: Venturing into the Amazon." *The Washington Post,* eight-part series starting December 13, 1981.

Gould, E. M., Jr., "The Future of Forests in Society." *The Forestry Chronicle,* December 1964.

Grainger, Alan, "The Shape of Woods to Come." *New Scientist,* April 2, 1981.

Hall, F. Keith, "Wood Pulp." *Scientific American,* April 1974.

Heinrichs, Jay, "Breeding Dixie's 'Supertrees.' " *American Forests,* December 1980.

Hileman, Bette:
"Acid Precipitation." *Environmental Science & Technology,* October 10, 1981.
"1982 Stockholm Conference on Acidification of the Environment." *Environmental Science & Technology,* Vol. 17, No. 1, 1983.

Hsiung, Wen-yue, and Frederic D. Johnson, "Forests and Forestry in China." *Journal of Forestry,* February 1981.

Hubscher, Françoise, "Sauver la Forêt Tropicale." *Ça M'Intéresse,* February 1983.

Hunter, Serena C., "Chaparral Fires: Are They Inevitable?" *American Forests,* September 1981.

Iker, Sam, "Islands of Life in a Forest Sea." *Mosaic,* September/October 1982.

Joyce, Christopher, "Tree-Saving Plant Struggles to Make the News." *New Scientist,* April 29, 1982.

Kinkead, Gwen, "Trouble in D. K. Ludwig's Jungle." *Fortune,* April 20, 1981.

Lewis, Henry T., "Indian Fires of Spring." *Natural History,* January 1980.

Likens, G. E., et al., "Recovery of a Deforested Ecosystem." *Science,* February 3, 1978.

Loudon, Andrew, "Too Many Deer for the Trees?" *New Scientist,* March 18, 1982.

"Ludwig's Wild Amazon Kingdom." *Time,* November 15, 1976.

McIntyre, Loren, "Amazon: The River Sea." *National Geographic,* October 1972.

Nadkarni, Nalini M., "Canopy Roots: Convergent Evolution in Rainforest Nutrient Cycles." *Science,* November 27, 1981.

Orville, Richard E., "Photograph of a Close Lightning Flash." *Science,* November 8, 1968.

Packer, James S., "Slash and Burn below the Border." *Smithsonian,* April 1973.

Page, Jake, "Woodman, Spare That Tree." *Science 82,* April.

Pearce, Fred, "The Menace of Acid Rain." *New Scientist,* August 12, 1982.

Perry, Donald:
"An Arboreal Naturalist Explores the Rain Forest's Mysterious Canopy." *Smithsonian,* June 1980.
"Lives of a Tree: The Mysterious Inner World of Tropical Plants." *Horticulture,* October 1977.

Raven, Peter H., "Tropical Rain Forests: A Global Responsibility." *Natural History,* February 1981.

Rothschild, Miriam, "Mimicry: The Deceptive Way of Life." *Natural History,* February 1967.

Sage, Bryan, "Conservationists Attack Britain's Forestry Plans." *New Scientist,* December 6, 1979.

Sanchez, Pedro A., et al., "Amazon Basin Soils: Management for Continuous Crop Production." *Science,* May 21, 1982.

Sibley, George, "Steam Donkeys, Tree Monkeys and Menzi Mucks." *Technology Illustrated,* April/May 1982.

Smith, Nigel J. H., "Colonization Lessons from a Tropical Forest." *Science,* November 13, 1981.

Spears, John S., "Can Farming and Forestry Coexist in the Tropics?" *Unasylva,* Vol. 32, No. 128, 1980.

Spurgeon, David, "The Promise of Agroforestry." *American Forests,* October 1980.

Spurr, Stephen H., "Silviculture." *Scientific American,* February 1979.

Stansell, John, "More Light Than Heat." *New Scientist,* August 20, 1981.

Sutcliffe, James, "Sap in the Treetops." *New Scientist,* June 11, 1981.

Tomlinson, P. B., "Tree Architecture." *American Scientist,* March/April 1983.

Tooker, Dorothy, "Most Ancient of Forests." *The Conservationist,* January/February 1981.

"Transamazonia: The Last Frontier." *Time,* September 13, 1971.

Uhl, Christopher, "You *Can* Keep A Good Forest Down." *Natural History,* April 1983.

Unasylva, Vol. 28, Nos. 112-113, 1976.

Van Der Spaa, David, "Jari: A Billion Dollar Gamble." *National Geographic,* May 1980.

Vogelmann, Hubert W., "Catastrophe on Camels Hump." *Natural History,* November 1982.

White, Peter T., "The Temples of Angkor: Ancient Glory in Stone." *National Geographic,* May 1982.

Wiegner, Kathleen K., "America's Green Gold." *Forbes,* December 24, 1979.

Williams, Keith, "Why Wood Is Not for Burning." *New Scientist,* October 15, 1981.

Wolff, Jack, "Today's Effort for Tomorrow's Timber." *American Horticulturist,* Fall 1978.

Zimmerman, Martin H.:
"How Sap Moves in Trees." *Scientific American,* March 1963.
"Piping Water to the Treetops." *Natural History,* July 1982.

Zobel, Bruce J., "The Genetic Improvement of Southern Pines." *Scientific American,* November 1971.

Other Publications

Anderson, Hal E., "Sundance Fire: An Analysis of Fire Phenomena." Research Paper INT-56, U.S. Department of Agriculture Forest Service, 1968.

Barney, Gerald O., study dir., *The Global 2000 Report to the President: Entering the Twenty-First Century.* Council on Environmental Quality and the Department of State, 1980.

"Defoliation by the Gypsy Moth: How It Hurts Your Tree." U.S. Department of Agriculture, Home and Garden Bulletin No. 223.

Eckholm, Erik, "Planting for the Future: Forestry for Human Needs." Worldwatch Paper 26, February 1979.

"Fire and the Forest: Taming Wildfire and Using Tame Fire." U.S. Department of Agriculture Forest Service, 1970.

"Forest Interpreter's Primer on Fire Management." Pamphlet TT-53 (1660/2300), U.S. Department of Agriculture Forest Service.

"Forestry for Rural Communities." Food and Agriculture Organization of the United Nations, No. 1/L6240/E/2/79/2/5000, February 1979.

Harland, W. B., et al., eds., "The Fossil Record. A Symposium with Documentation." London: Geological Society of London, 1967.

Harris, Larry D., et al., "The Development of Silviculture Systems for Wildlife." IMPAC Report, October 1979.

"History of Smokejumping." Aviation and Fire Management, U.S. Department of Agriculture Forest Service, No. R1-80-22, August 1, 1980.

Katzenstein, Alan W., "An Updated Perspective on Acid Rain." Edison Electric Institute Acid Rain Public Response Task Force, November 1981.

Little, Elbert L., Jr., "Checklist of United States Trees (Native and Naturalized)." U.S. Department of Agriculture Forest Service Agriculture Handbook No. 541, September 1979.

Lotan, James E., et al., "Effects of Fire on Flora: A State-of-Knowledge Review." U.S. Department of Agriculture Forest Service General Technical Report WO-16, 1978.

"National Forest Fire Report, 1981." U.S. Department of Agriculture Forest Service, August 1982.

Perkins, Thomas W., "Paleontological Contributions: Textures and Conditions of Formation of Middle Pennsylvanian Coal Balls, Central United States." University of Kansas Paleontological Institute, Paper 82, UKPCA 82 1-13 (1976), April 30, 1976.

Perry, Donald R., and Sylvia E. Merschel, "Life in the Jungle Canopy." *1981 Yearbook of Science and the Future*, Encyclopaedia Britannica, 1982.

"Petrified Forests of Yellowstone." U.S. Department of the Interior Handbook 108. Division of Publications, National Park Service, 1980.

Phillips, Tom L., et al., "Fossil Peat of the Illinois Basin: A Guide to the Study of Coal Balls of Pennsylvanian Age." Illinois State Geological Survey, 1976.

"The Scientific Base for Silviculture and Management Decisions in the National Forest System: Selected Papers." U.S. Department of Agriculture Forest Service, 1977.

Vietmeyer, Noel D., "Leucaena: New Hope for the Tropics." *Yearbook of Science and the Future,* Encyclopaedia Britannica, 1978.

"Wildfire: A Story of Modern Firefighting." U.S. Department of Agriculture Forest Service, No. PA 993.

PICTURE CREDITS

The sources for the illustrations that appear in this book are listed below. Credits for the illustrations from left to right are separated by semicolons; from top to bottom they are separated by dashes.

Cover: Jeff Gnass. 6, 7: © Tom Bean. 8, 9: Glenn Van Nimwegen © 1974; Heather Angel, Surrey, England. 10, 11: Takeshi Ohta, Tsuruoka, Yamagata Prefecture. 12, 13: Dennis Brokaw; Tad Nichols. 14, 15: W. H. Hodge from Peter Arnold, Inc. 16: USDA Forest Service. 19: Dr. Richard E. Orville. 20: Hal E. Anderson from USDA Forest Service. 22, 23: USDA Forest Service. 25: Jan Taylor from Bruce Coleman Ltd., Middlesex, England. 27, 28: USDA Forest Service. 29: Cliff Winfield, Perth, Western Australia. 30, 31: Wayne Adkins from Southeastern Forest Experiment Station. 34, 35: Anthony P. Gomez from USDA Forest Service. 36, 37: Jim Hughes from USDA Forest Service. 38, 39: G. R. Roberts, Nelson, New Zealand. 40, 41: John C. Jones © 1980. 42, 43: Jeffrey P. Cutting, Canberra, Australia, inset, Jeffrey P. Cutting, Canberra, courtesy Department of Forestry, Queensland, Australia. 44: Courtesy Smithsonian Institution. 46: Courtesy New York State Museum, Albany. 49: Bob Clemenz Photography. 50: M.P.L. Fogden from Bruce Coleman Ltd., Middlesex, England—Arnold Holeywell. 52, 53: Illustrations by Richard Crist. 55: Jeff Gnass. 56: Richard Rowan; Heather Angel, Surrey, England—Schapowalow/Zölck, Hamburg. 57: ZEFA, Düsseldorf—Betty Crowell. 58: Charlie Ott from Bruce Coleman Ltd., Middlesex, England; Fulco Pratesi from Delta Photos, Rome. 59: Courtesy Smithsonian Institution. 62: G. R. Roberts, Nelson, New Zealand; Tui De Roy Moore, Galapagos, Ecuador. 63: J.R.P. van Hoey Smith, Rotterdam; © Bruce A. Macdonald from Earth Scenes—G. R. Roberts, Nelson, New Zealand; Heather Angel, Surrey, England. 65: Tui De Roy Moore, Galapagos, Ecuador. 66-69: Art by Lloyd K. Townsend. 70: Heather Angel, Surrey, England. 73: © Klaus D. Francke, Hamburg. 75: M.P.L. Fogden from Bruce Coleman, Inc.; Ed Cooper. 76: Norman Owen Tomalin from Bruce Coleman, Inc.; Jack Dermid; Betty Crowell—Heather Angel, Surrey, England; Ed Cooper; John Shaw from Bruce Coleman, Inc. 77: P. Raba from ZEFA, Düsseldorf; Jack Dermid; Norman Owen Tomalin from Bruce Coleman, Inc.—Department of Forestry, Queensland, Australia; Eric Crichton from Bruce Coleman Ltd., Middlesex, England (2). 79: Runk/Schoenberger from Grant Heilman Photography; John de Visser from Masterfile—© David Alan Harvey from Woodfin Camp, Inc. 81-83: Art by Trudy Nicholson. 85: Thomas W. Martin from Photo Researchers. 87: Wilfred A. Côté, Jr. and Arnold C. Day. 88: N. C. Brown Center for Ultrastructure Studies, SUNY College of Environmental Science and Forestry—Dr. Joan Nowicke, courtesy Smithsonian Institution; Dr. J. H. Troughton, New Zealand Department of Scientific and Industrial Research and F. B. Sampson, Victoria University, Wellington. 89: N. C. Brown Center for Ultrastructure Studies, SUNY College of Environmental Science and Forestry. 91: Heather Angel, Surrey, England. 92, 93: Dennis Brokaw. 94, 95: Ed Cooper; G. Phillipart de Foy from Explorer, Paris. 96: Mexican Tourism Secretariat, Mexico City—Hummel from ZEFA, Düsseldorf. 97: Department of Forestry, Queensland, Australia. 98, 99: Betty Crowell; Peter Guttman. 100: Betty Crowell—Steve Crouch © 1978. 101: W. H. Hodge from Peter Arnold, Inc. 102: Jeff Gnass. 104: Map by Bill Hezlep. 106: Grant Heilman Photography. 107: Richard Rowan. 108, 109: Metsäkuva-Arkisto Ky, Helsinki. 110, 111: Walter Chandoha. 112, 113: © David Falconer. 114, 115: Alex S. MacLean © 1980. 116: M.P.L. Fogden from Bruce Coleman Ltd., Middlesex, England. 117: Runk/Schoenberger from Grant Heilman Photography. 118: Bild der Wissenschaft, Weinert, Stuttgart. 120: Günter Ziesler, Munich. 123: Map by Bill Hezlep. 124, 125: Cheryl Pick © 1980 from After-Image. 126: Donald R. Perry © 1980. 127: Peter Ward from Bruce Coleman Ltd., Middlesex, England. 128: M.P.L. Fogden from Bruce Coleman Ltd., Middlesex, England; Robin Hanbury-Tenison from Robert Harding Picture Library, London—© Zig Lescz from Animals Animals—Hans Pfletschinger, © Toni Angermayer, Holzkirchen; Robin Hanbury-Tenison from Robert Harding Picture Library, London. 129: M.P.L. Fogden from Bruce Coleman Ltd., Middlesex, England, except upper right, Donald R. Perry © 1980. 131: Victor Englebert. 132, 133: Michel Huet-HOA-QUI, Paris; © Brian J. Coates from Bruce Coleman Ltd., Middlesex, England—Heather Angel, Surrey, England. 134-138: Donald R. Perry. 140, 141: Takashi Yoshida, Tokyo; Martin Rogers © 1979 from Woodfin Camp, Inc. 142-147: Loren McIntyre. 148: Schapowalow/Albinger, Hamburg. 150, 151: Courtesy Weyerhaeuser Co. 152: Courtesy Weyerhaeuser Co.; Metsäkuva-Arkisto Ky, Helsinki—Michael Wotton (2). 153: American Forest Institute. 154, 155: G. R. Roberts, Nelson, New Zealand. 156: Metsäkuva-Arkisto Ky, Helsinki; © Forestry Commission, Edinburgh, Scotland. 159: David Falconer from After-Image. 160: G. R. Roberts, Nelson, New Zealand. 161: Myrleen Ferguson © 1982. 163: Galen Rowell. 164, 165: Florita Botts, F.A.O., Rome. 166-169: Marcella Pedone, Milan.

INDEX

174